"Inspiring, direct, courageous, powerful, and timely. Hatmaker 'gets it' and gives the modern-day church a wake-up call. This 'how to' book will certainly encourage anyone who feels, and is willing to embrace, the tension in this call. If you want to join the amazing, scary, awesome, engaging, adventurous, dangerous, passionate and rewarding journey God has in store for you, read this book."

—Caroline M. Boudreaux, Founder,
The Miracle Foundation

"Brandon Hatmaker reveals the bridge that links worship and mission and proves how our life becomes authentic to the world and acceptable to God only by having one foot firmly planted on each shore. Brandon is a prophetic voice who leads us out of the guilt-laden, often overwhelming notions of what we should be doing as Christians, and he shows us the redeeming, life-giving work God has for each of us in a world that 'waits in groaning' for hope, love, and rescue. Don't miss this book!"

—Andy Hein, Church Mobilization Director,
International Justice Mission.

"This book contains a lot of heart, mixed with a good dose of authenticity, and spiced with a fair bit of courage. Brandon offers us an articulate vision of a church that lives true to her calling to be God's agents of change in a broken world. Bring it on!"

—Alan Hirsch, founder of Forge Mission Training Network
and author of *The Forgotten Ways*, *On The Verge*,
The Faith of Leap, and others.

"Refreshing. Powerful. Needed. Brandon connects the dots with both philosophic and practical steps to effective impact. Read this and get ready to change."

—Jeremie Kubicek, CEO of GiANT Impact, which owns Catalyst
and author of national bestseller *Leadership Is Dead*.

"Through the stories of his time at Austin New Church, Brandon shares his heart for seeing Austin — and the world — transformed. *Barefoot Church* succeeds in giving the reader real, practical ideas for renewal."

—Matt Carter, Pastor of Preaching & Vision,
The Austin Stone Community Church

"From a deep well of experience, Brandon exposes and then calls us toward a faith that Jesus calls 'PURE!' *Barefoot Church* is the message of God to the church, to its leaders, and to you. If this book gets under your skin, everything changes!"

—Hugh Halter, author of *AND* and *The Tangible Kingdom*

"*Barefoot Church* should be every church. Brandon Hatmaker hits the issues on the head and then lives it out in his church. This is not a theoretical book. It will certainly disappoint anyone who is interested in a 'good read' about church but disinterested in changing the way they 'do church.' It is one that is lived out day by day through Austin New Church where Brandon serves, which is a Barefoot Church indeed. In a day when so many talk about the need to be authentic, accessible to the world, and loving in tangible ways, Brandon lays it out simply, convincingly and with conviction."

—Matthew A. Thomas, Bishop,
Free Methodist Church of North America

"*Barefoot Church* is not a book of theory. It reflects the life of one of America's real, on-the-ground, first-world missionary couples. It's a fantastic call to mission and an inspiring paradigm-shifting book to give anyone who says they are followers of Jesus. Brandon challenges pastors, leaders, and every member of the church to action. As someone involved in training people to be on mission, this is a book I would put in the hands of every Forge America resident."

—Kim Hammond, National Director of Forge America.

"In *Barefoot Church*, you'll be challenged to live out the whole gospel in every part of your life. Brandon Hatmaker lays out a theology for helping the underresourced and tells inspiring stories while helping to change the scorecard for the church to live out its mission. If you're serious about living a sent life and sending others, you will want to read *Barefoot Church*."

—Dave Ferguson, lead pastor of Community Christian Church, Spiritual Entrepreneur, NewThing

BAREFOOT**CHURCH**

EXPONENTIAL
series

BAREFOOT CHURCH

SERVING THE LEAST IN A CONSUMER CULTURE

BRANDON HATMAKER

ZONDERVAN®

EXPONENTIAL
network

Leadership Network

ZONDERVAN.com/
AUTHORTRACKER
follow your favorite authors

ZONDERVAN

Barefoot Church
Copyright © 2011 by Brandon Hatmaker

This title is also available as a Zondervan ebook. Visit www.zondervan.com/ebooks.

This title is also available in a Zondervan audio edition. Visit www.zondervan.fm.

Requests for information should be addressed to:
Zondervan, *Grand Rapids, Michigan 49530*

Library of Congress Cataloging-in-Publication Data

Hatmaker, Brandon, 1972-.
    Barefoot church : serving the least in a consumer culture / Brandon Hatmaker.
        p.   cm. —(Exponential series)
    ISBN 978-0-310-49226-9 (softcover)
    1. Church work with the poor. I. Title.
BV639.P6H38   2011
259.086'942—dc23   2011023735

Cover design: Rob Monacelli
Interior illustration: Rob Monacelli
Interior design: Sherri L. Hoffman

Printed in the United States of America

12 13 14 15 16 17 18 /DCI/ 22 21 20 19 18 17 16 15 14 13 12 11 10 9 8 7 6 5

To Jesus and Jen. This was your fault. I love you both even more because of it. Jesus, I pray this is of you and for you. Jen, you have the toughest job in the world, dealing with me. Thank you both for letting me try stuff, fail, rant, rave, process, and somehow come out the other end a little further along the road.

CONTENTS

FOREWORD

Then Jesus asked, "What is the kingdom of God like?"
LUKE 13:18a

Jesus spent much of his earthly ministry teaching about God's kingdom. He taught how that kingdom was different from the kingdoms of the Persians, Assyrians, or Romans—the kingdoms with which his listeners were most familiar. The ethics of the kingdom, the teaching that formed the substance of the Sermon on the Mount, sharply contrasted with the "here-and-now" focus of this life, and his words were like a bright light in the darkness, exposing the hidden sin behind the ritualistic religion that had developed from the law. Using parables, Jesus taught and explained the nuances of his kingdom, clarifying his Father's role and his own part in bringing about the coming kingdom. Using children as examples, he illustrated to his listeners the type of faith that would mark citizens of the kingdom of heaven (Luke 18:16). And using a model prayer, he spoke of the kingdom's eternal nature (Matt. 6:13).

After Jesus was betrayed and arrested, he was asked by the Roman governor, Pontius Pilate, if he was a king. He responded by saying that his kingdom was *not* "of this world," adding this clarification: "If it were, my servants would fight" (John 18:36). The normal path to power and authority necessitated the taking up of arms in open rebellion. One of Jesus' disciples, Peter, had already started down that path, cutting off the ear of the high priest's servant in the garden. Peter's violent response, though well-intended, received a rebuke from Christ, who healed the servant and willingly surrendered to the Roman authorities. Jesus was making it clear that his goal was not the violent overthrow of the Roman occupation or the pursuit of political and military rule. His intention was far more subversive.

His goal was to change the world — forever.

Jesus established his church and empowered his followers at Pentecost, unleashing the life-changing power of God on an unsuspecting world. Since that time, his followers have continued to effect change by bearing witness to the life, death, and resurrection of Jesus. The visual manifestation of Jesus' kingdom rule — his church — would become the living example of the kingdom that the prophets of God had intoned in generations past. The kingdom of God was inaugurated into this world through the incarnation of God's Son in the person of Jesus Christ. Through his rule, the kingdom would now be extended by the mission of the church, reaching every corner of creation and overcoming spiritual darkness until the day of Christ's return.

In contrast to the prevailing pattern of the culture since the days of Babel and Noah, the church was *different*—a community called to combat greed with contentment, lust with love, brutality with kindness, and power-grabbing with humble service. Instead of conquering through might, the kingdom, like yeast, would gradually infiltrate the nations of the world. The power of God was demonstrated in the gospel, which redeemed and transformed the enemies of God's kingdom into its holy citizens.

In this book, Brandon Hatmaker issues a clear call to the church: to remember her practical, spiritual heritage as the visible manifestation of God's kingdom rule. He reminds us that the most world-changing work we do may not be in the halls of governmental power, but rather, among the poor, the homeless, and those who are victims of injustice. He draws our attention to some of the weaknesses of the church in our Western culture—how being Christ to the poor can easily become just another ministry on top of our other programs, worship services, small groups, and Bible studies. The church has forgotten the incisive words of Jesus in the parable of the sheep and the goats: that Jesus is most likely to be found among the poor, the hungry, the unclothed, and the imprisoned—not necessarily in the places of worldly power: Congressional offices, court rooms, or the hallowed halls of the White House.

And lest we assume that Hatmaker's call is just another salvo in the missional/attractional, traditional/contemporary, liturgical/hang-from-the-light-fixtures war of words, he quickly dispels that notion: "*Barefoot Church* is not about attractional, seeker-sensitive, culturally relevant, or other models. It is not a church growth strategy or new style of church. Contrary to popular belief, serving the least does not make a missional church. It's about serving the least *and* your neighbor. It's about balancing the fasting *and* the feast. It's about making the altar both a place for communion *and* a place to leave your shoes."

The gospel of Jesus Christ, embodied and proclaimed by the church, remains the only hope of the world, which means it is also the only hope of the poor and disenfranchised. To be the body of Christ, we would do well to remember that our bare feet, rather than being adorned with Gucci's and Jimmy Choo's, need only be dressed with the gospel of peace, a gospel through which lives will be changed, not the least of which will be our own.

Ed Stetzer, president of LifeWay Research,

www.edstetzer.com;

author of *Transformational Church* and *Compelled by Love*

ACKNOWLEDGMENTS

Thank you, Jesus, for finishing the story. Now we can focus on the journey. We're better there; if left up to us, we'd ruin the ending. Give us the wisdom to understand and the courage to follow.

Jen, you are my hero. My greatest joy has been serving shoulder to shoulder with you. You're an amazing woman of God, wife, mother, author, teacher, and friend. And you're smokin' hot (bonus). I love you deeply.

Thanks Tray & Jenny, Matthew & Sarah, Lamar & Jill, John & Audrey, as well as the rest of the Austin New Church family. I wish I could name you all. There are no words. You are the church we dreamed of.

Thanks to all those involved with Restore Austin and the Austin PlantR Network. I can't imagine serving in a city without such a great network of leaders, dreamers, and planters.

To Hugh and Matt at Missio and Adullam, thanks for pioneering something most of us were afraid of. Thanks for saying things others are afraid to say. Thanks for believing in what we're doing enough to be an advocate. And thanks for your friendship.

To Dennis, Tom, Matt, and everyone at The River Conference and the FMC, thanks for believing in us, for dreaming with us, and for sacrificing and loving us along the way.

Thanks to everyone at Leadership Network, Zondervan, and Exponential. Your visionary leadership has a greater impact than you know. Thanks for leading the way.

CHAPTER 1

There's Got to Be More

Recently, my wife, Jen, and I were having an all-too-familiar conversation with a young couple who had given up on church. Not a specific church, *the* church. While both of them had attended since birth and had even served a few years in ministry, they had become jaded and joined the ranks of those claiming, "Church—as we see it—is not for us."

They had experienced a myriad of what they considered painful church experiences. Every time they gave it another try, church seemed to lose credibility, trust was broken, and relationships were abused. For years they desperately sought how to navigate the waters of their tension. Yet they had come to the conclusion that in their search for more, as the church remained the same, so did they.

When given a chance to share specifics on the thing that "what's-his-name" had said or what "so-and-so" had done, the young wife exploded passionately with a single-themed indictment: "The church needs to care more about the poor! They need to fight injustice! They need to help the orphan and widow in their distress! They need to do what they say they're about!"

Silence.

Surprising even herself, and with a slightly stunned look on her face, she calmly said as a tear rolled down her cheek, "Here's the problem: I don't do it either. I don't know how. I don't even know where to start."

That was a big moment for me. It's easy to cast stones. It's easy to point out the problems in the existing church. And it's just as easy to pretend we're not a part of the problem. But this was a refreshingly honest confession of ownership that I've come to find so many believers identifying with. They want to do something of more significance, but they don't even know where to start.

We as church leaders tell our people to go. We tell them to be good news. And we assume they do. We assume they know how. While we've been charged to "equip the saints" for works of service, the brutal truth is that most of us have reduced our expectations of "serving" to a once-a-month tour of duty as an usher or greeter. We've settled for serving ourselves and serving as an event rather than serving those in need and living a new way of life that Jesus has called us to.

There's got to be more to church than this.

This book tells the story of how a church that prioritizes serving the least was formed, and how among the least they actually found more. Although our story happened while planting Austin New Church (ANC), my purpose isn't to give you a model for church planting. Rather, it's to share principles we've found helpful in equipping believers to live outside themselves. I'll offer practical ideas for creating service-based, missional communities that end up being surprisingly as much about evangelism, discipleship, and real-life transformation as they are about serving others. We'll take a look at how the organizational structure of church can be created and even restructured for mission in any context. And by the end, I hope to demonstrate how any church can truly be a catalyst for individual, collective, and social renewal.

More than anything, this book is about a Christ-centered gospel. By his example and through his teaching, my hope is that we are continuously being challenged to be good news to a lost, broken, and dying world. That God would open our eyes more and more each day to the needs of our community and world. That we would see it as the church's responsibility to lead the charge in making a difference, not just on our own church campus, but also in our neighborhoods, our workplaces, our city, our nation, and our world.

WHY A BAREFOOT CHURCH

God sent me on a journey that, to be honest, was not much fun. He was doing annoying things like confronting me with my own selfishness. He was pointing out the fact that my faith had morphed into religion, and after a Bible degree and a handful of years in full-time ministry, it had become way too "professional."

I was leading at the megachurch post of my dreams, with a multimillion-dollar budget, state-of-the-art facilities, a legion of programs, and an amazingly gifted staff; yet I was in a personal rut. I was dry. While I had literally given all that I had to the church, I had lost the joy of my calling. And I had no one to blame. I looked across the landscape of the American church and, in a brief moment of clarity, realized that I was a part of the problem. The application of my theology had become man-centric. My ministry had become more about me and my leadership than about God and his presence. My efforts were more about a self-absorbed faith than delivering good news to those in need. I had become a consumer Christian, and I was leading others to do the same.

> I looked across the landscape of the American church, and in a brief moment of clarity, realized that I was a part of the problem.

Whose fault was it? Which came first, the consumer Christian or the consumer church? Was it the chicken or the egg? Honestly, it didn't matter. I was both.

God didn't offer the courtesy of easing me into dealing with my self-centered faith. It was a full-frontal attack. It was as if he said, "Okay, Brandon, now I'm going to take everything you know and turn it on its ear."

I want you to leave the security of your current position and start over.

I want you to learn what it means to serve the poor and lead others to do the same.

I want you to discover what I'm doing in my kingdom and be a part of it.

> Me: "What? Resign my position? Who will pay my bills? I am completely dependent on my job, I have too much debt, and I just remodeled my kitchen."
>
> God: "I know."
>
> Me: "Serve the poor? I don't even know any."
>
> God: "Exactly."
>
> Me: "Your kingdom? Honestly, God, don't tell anyone this, but I'm not sure I know what that even means."
>
> God: "You will."

So I prayed. Initially—yes, I admit it—I prayed that God would just leave me alone. The problem was that he already had my wife on his side, so I was outnumbered. But I knew he was serious. I had never been so scared in my life. So, out of complete and absolute fear that God would remove his hand from my life, my family, and my ministry, I asked him to offer evidence that this directive was really from him, and I begged for a vision of what this might look like.

At first, I thought God might be calling me to start a nonprofit organization that served the poor. So far, those were the only marching orders I had been given. I wondered if I would have to leave occupational ministry in order to commit fully to serve those in physical need. I hope you see the irony in that. But at the time that was the direction God seemed to be leading me. From the moment I started taking this seriously, God used random people from the homeless community to send me messages so obvious, it was almost obnoxious.

In this context the vision came.

It was a freakishly cold Easter Sunday in Austin, Texas. What might normally have been a day of sunshine and mid-70s (causing an intuitive basking on the patio of a downtown coffee shop while sipping on a cup of joe) had turned into a bundled-up day of freezing temperatures.

After plowing through six Easter services at my current church, Jen and I decided to finish the day in anonymity by attending a gathering that evening at a small, socially active church downtown. We had been considering what God was doing in our lives for a few months and were praying for clarity on how it might fit into our current context. It's amazing how hungry we had become for God when we were desperate to hear from him.

Worship was incredible that night. I'm not sure that it was really technically all that great; I just know I was hungry for a word from God and was worshiping my guts out, so it seemed great. As I closed my eyes during a song, I had what I guess some might call a vision. It wasn't something that had ever happened to me, so it messed with me a bit. I saw myself walking down the main drag outside this downtown church when I heard a homeless man say to me, "Give me your boots."

Time out.

This was an interesting request to me. Not the demand itself, but the fact that Jen and I were both wearing cowboy boots that we had just bought each other for Christmas. They cost about four times as much as any other pair of shoes I had ever owned. They weren't even broken in yet, and they were sweet. Typically, we might have been wearing a nice ten-dollar pair of flip-flops that evening, but the freezing weather had everyone donning shoes and boots.

My response to this imaginary homeless man's request? While my heart said, "You're crazy, these are my good boots," my mouth simply made excuses and blurted out, "They won't fit you."

To which he quickly replied with confidence, "Oh, they'll fit."

That was it. No flashing light. No clear orders for what to do next. No music in the background and a continued vision of me taking my boots off (in slow motion, of course) and handing them to him with his child peeking around the corner saying, "Daddy, that man sure is a good Christian."

Nope. That was it. So I kept singing.

Shane Claiborne was speaking that night. It was the first time I had heard him speak, and it was pretty convicting. He shared stories from when he had spent a year with Mother Teresa at Calcutta. He spoke about the faith community he was a part of in Philadelphia. Then he closed by telling us about the church he was at that morning in San Antonio that had a large homeless population as a part of their membership.

He had asked about their greatest need. They said they were in need of really good shoes, and even more so, quality boots. Since they were on their feet most of the day and their primary mode of transportation was walking, they went through shoes like crazy. That and the fact that most people donate only either cheap shoes or old shoes made the need for quality shoes and boots much more significant.

As Shane was closing out his time of teaching and began to set up a time of communion, he mentioned that we were going to do something a little different. He said that if God led us, and only if God was really leading us, we were to take off our shoes and as we came forward to take communion, place them on the altar, and he would take them to this homeless community the next day.

I was stunned. First by my selfishness — that with all I had been through, I was secretly wishing I had worn cheaper shoes. And second, once it sunk in, how humbling it was to hear God speak. That he was really moving in our lives. That he was speaking to us tangibly and undeniably. And that once again, I was confronted with the reality that he cared way more about those in need than I did.

As we placed our boots on the altar, I might have cried a little (a lot). The Spirit was thick. Everything about that moment was right. And I wished that I could just bottle that place in time and keep it forever. It was obvious that there was something in what we were experiencing that we were supposed to do.

It was later that night that we felt God communicated where he was leading us. I still remember what it felt like when my bare feet hit the cold concrete outside of that downtown building. It feels like just yesterday that I turned around to look up the stairs and saw an entire church being sent out into a city ... barefoot.

It was clear what Jesus was saying: "This is how I want my church to look, a place where love and self-sacrifice are hardwired into the DNA of my people, of solidarity with the poor — a true community rallied around my gospel. I want a church where the altar is not only a place to take communion but also a place to leave your shoes. I want a barefoot church."

MAKING IT PERSONAL

A few weeks later, after a few more unexplainable "God" moments and some hours spent volunteering downtown with the homeless community, I was standing on my front lawn absorbing our impending journey. I realized for the first time I was really beginning to care about the homeless. I never had. I had always seen them as lazy, most likely criminals, and probably drug addicts. But after serving for several weeks, I began to put names with faces and hear stories that could derail any of us. I began to realize that my stereotype was not only unfair, but it was untrue. My heart had begun to change toward them. Bottom line, I was changing. Finally. It was incredibly refreshing.

Right at that moment, I was distracted by my neighbor's lawn. It was about knee high, and it was annoying. The only thing more annoying than their grass was their landscaping. The only thing more annoying than their landscaping was the worn-out tire marks in the middle of the lawn where their twenty-four-year-old son (who still lived at home) parked when he came home in the middle of the night.

I quickly became distracted from my noble, righteous journey, and my pious thoughts were replaced with judgment and disdain. I live in a really nice neighborhood; why in the world do I always seem to end up living next to the only house that looks like this?

God: "That really bugs you, doesn't it?"

Me: "Heck yeah, it does. What did I ever do to deserve this?"

God: "Why don't you do something about it?"

Me: "Why would I? It's not my lawn."

God: "Because she's a widow who lost her husband five years ago to cancer, and she doesn't know how to start a lawn mower. Because she's got a loser son who takes advantage of her day after day. Because not only are you a Christian, you're a pastor. Because you're so self-consumed that you didn't even see her need, and this is exactly what you need to do to change your heart."

Okay, maybe God didn't call her son a loser. That was me. But he certainly made his point. So I got out my lawn mower and started cutting. And I wept. Again. Even harder than I did at the altar where I gave my boots. And I did it every week—both cut her lawn and cried. It took a whole five minutes. Quite the sacrifice! God made his point.

One day, I noticed a plate of homemade cookies sitting by my front door. With it was a note from my neighbor that read, "Brandon, I just don't know what I'm going to do with you. Thank you so much for cutting my grass. I only hope one day I can repay you for your kindness."

She already did. I've been paid back sevenfold.

Mother Teresa lived by a belief that there is physical, emotional, and spiritual need in every community.

Mother Teresa lived by a belief that there is physical, emotional, and spiritual need in every community. Need is everywhere, yet we too often fail to see it. If we don't see it, we won't be bothered by it. If we're not bothered by it, we won't engage it. By our neglect, we become the oppressor.

Jesus knew exactly what he was doing when he told us to serve the least. He knew that if we would serve them, we would become agents of change. Despair would change to hope. The reputation of his bride would change. And along the way, our hearts and minds would change. We need that in the church today.

SOMETHING MUST CHANGE

Prior to starting Austin New Church, I spent a lot of time with pastor friends from the community trying to see where God was at work. I told them a little about my journey and that I felt God was calling us to do something that focused primarily on serving the least. My hope was to find some counsel on where we could start and what it might look like as a part of what God was already doing in our city.

I found myself talking to a frustrated pastor one day who shared his vision about the message series they were about to do on social justice. It was a six-week series with some intentional action steps toward getting their people out of their comfort zone and into the world to serve. Most of what they were doing would be accomplished through their small groups. Sounded great and incredibly affirming to me.

But what he quickly found is that the structure of their church did not support the vision for serving. Instead, it ended up being just one more thing that the people felt took up their time. Everyone complained that they were just too busy with church, small groups, and Bible study to add another day a month to serve the poor.

Many of us want to be more outward and service focused, but we find ourselves bound by a structure that just doesn't allow room for it.

Later, I saw that the series was reduced to a one-weekend awareness push. And their service projects were replaced with a one-time love offering.

This is a shared frustration among pastors. Many of us want to be more outward and service focused, but we find ourselves bound by a structure that just doesn't allow room for it. We either created it or have tolerated it. So what do we do when we know it's a neglected biblical reality in our life or ministry, we have a renewed passion for serving those in need, we realize that this is an increasingly important passion of the emerging generations, and yet all of us (and our people) are already so busy we can't even imagine when we'd actually do it?

Some of us need an organizational tweak, some a structural overhaul, but there's one hard truth we all have to hear: all movement toward mission requires sacrifice. Nothing of great value comes without great cost. That said, there's hope for the church. There always is. While we'll talk more about making change a reality in the coming chapters, especially on how to reorganize in simple ways, here's a critical and evaluative starting point.

Craig Van Gelder wrote in his book *The Ministry of the Missional Church*:

> The Church is.
> The Church does what it is.
> The Church organizes what it does.[1]

Each of us claims our church "is" something. We think our church is known by a specific vision or mission. Maybe we hope that what our church "is" is captured by our mission statement or strategic initiatives.

But it's the church's calling to the gospel and God's mission that provide the framework for its ministry. The mission determines what we "do," and what we "do" requires organization that functions in support of the mission. This goes beyond simply modifying our behavior and calls us toward a new identity in Christ.

Here's something to consider: we may say we're a church on mission, yet we have so many on-campus programs that our people never have time to live on mission in their neighborhoods. We may say we're more than just a Sunday service, but 90 percent of our resources and efforts are either committed to the Sunday morning experience or events designed to draw people to our buildings. We may think we serve, but if we took an honest look, we'd find only a small percentage of our people actually serving outside the church.

Do we have the structure in place to support what we want to do and what we want to be known for? If you're a pastor, are you willing to organize and reorganize your budget, your staff, your priorities, your evaluations, and your calendars to reflect that vision? If you're a layperson reading this book and believe something needs to change, are you willing to be a part of the solution? Are you willing to lay down the idols of "how we've always done it"? Are you willing to be changed yourself? Are you willing to partner with others to make bold moves in supporting this vision?

If not, then this dream is not really that important to us. Our faith is still about us — and we're fooling ourselves.

Washington Times religion editor Julia Duin shared in her recent book, *Quitting Church*, how astonishing it was to see how many pastors are in denial about what's going on in their own faith community. Those in leadership see things one way while others see them as they really are. The seeker sees the discrepancy. The skeptic sees it. And our members feel it. That's why they're leaving. They see it clearly. Everyone sees it except us. As Duin put it, "A lot of evangelical leaders (*simply*) do not see the problem."[2]

Maybe you see the problem. Maybe you're reading this book because you're ready for change. You're not alone.

Maybe you see the problem. Maybe you're reading this book because you're ready for change. You're not alone. There is certainly a revived spirit of service sweeping the hearts of believers today. This is a good thing. And it's bigger than we even know. Hopefully you're looking for some practical ways to begin changing what you see. More than likely, that will have to start with you and me. Let's stop complaining about the church we see and start becoming the church we dream of.[3]

Regardless of your reason for reading this book, regardless of what your dream church looks like, my prayer is that God will raise up in you a new and fresh passion for the church. I pray that you will feel an affirming movement of the Spirit when you consider taking your affections off yourself, placing them on people who have nothing to offer you, and leading others to do the same.

CLEARING THINGS UP

Barefoot Church is not about attractional, seeker-sensitive, culturally relevant, or other models. It is not a church growth strategy or
new style of church. Contrary to popular belief, serving the least does
not make a missional church. It's about serving the least *and* your
neighbor. It's about balancing the fasting *and* the feast. It's about
making the altar both a place for communion *and*
a place to leave your shoes. We can have confidence
in knowing that the hopes for each are close to the
heart of God. The question that remains is how
close it is to our heart. Each of us has the responsibility to navigate what serving the least looks like in
our life, in our context, and in our church.

> **Each of us has the responsibility to navigate what serving the least looks like in our life, in our context, and in our church.**

Missional and *attractional* are terms often heard
in church leadership today. Unfortunately their
overuse and blanket use can easily create more confusion than clarity. For our purposes we'll use the
word *missional* in this book to describe the sending or incarnational efforts of the church. Incarnation literally means to "put on flesh." Jesus was God incarnate.
He literally put on skin and dwelt among us. He moved into our
neighborhood and spoke our language. So when we say we are to
live incarnationally, we mean we are to "put on" Jesus and represent
him by focusing on being his hands and feet to our world. To live
on mission. This includes but is not limited to serving the least. It
might be a sending toward your neighbor or to a complete stranger
in need. Either way, the focus is essentially on the church becoming
missionaries to our culture.

We'll use the term *attractional* to refer primarily to the gathering
nature of the church. Often the idea of *attractional* manifests itself in
the form of exaltation, proclamation, and corporate worship. While I
believe an incarnational life is indeed attractive, we'll mostly use the
label *attractional* to refer to programs and events designed intentionally
to attract attenders to the church campus or to the location of an event.

Unfortunately, when it comes to programming and church structure, these terms are often viewed as opposing forces. That's understandable since they often utilize effort, time, people, and money from the same resource pool. But what I hope we'll come to see is that while they have two different purposes and priorities, it's by design that they actually work best together. Their beauty is not found in their existence, it's found in their coexistence: working in perfect harmony by taking the focus off ourselves and placing it where it ought to be—on God and on others.

Likewise, many terms and phrases have been used to describe what it means to serve the least. You'll see most of them in the pages of this book as well. Since each can have multiple definitions and have been used in many different ways, let's also take a moment to clarify our position on each of them.

"Serving the least" and "serving the poor" can describe any action or posture of benevolence or compassion to those considered underprivileged, marginalized, neglected, or oppressed. "The least" is a collective description of those in need. It describes anyone who simply has less. "Less" can refer to anything from being underresourced to being alone, from having inadequate or no housing to little or no food, from the rarity of comfort to the complete lack of freedom. Less is simply less.

"Serving the poor" primarily refers to those who are in physical need. Often the "poor" have an abundance of relational and spiritual support or love. Serving the poor locally is more often an offering of immediate relief. Serving the poor globally has a variety of implications and can easily be connected to human trafficking and slavery as much as it can to hunger or poor living conditions.

"Social action" and "social justice" are often used interchangeably. "Social action" focuses on the existence of a holistic concern and action regardless of its form. Simple acts of mercy, offering temporary relief, having compassion, and fighting for justice can all be described as social action. However, social action paints with broad strokes, while social justice tends to be more specific. "Social justice" often zeros in on efforts resulting in long-term societal change stemming from significant global needs.

"Mercy" and "justice" are themes found throughout Scripture and describe both the reason for and the methods of engaging need. "Mercy" is most often translated to mean kindness or goodness. It's the heart and motivation behind the action. It comes from a Hebrew word literally meaning to "bow the neck in courtesy; to be kind."[4] Its New Testament usage is often translated to mean compassion or pity.[5]

The Hebrew word for "justly," used primarily in the Old Testament, means a "verdict pronounced judicially."[6] The Greek word for "justice" in the New Testament means vengeance, vindication, or the avenging of wrong. Together we can gain a greater understanding of justice to mean to intentionally act justly or to proactively seek justice.[7]

> We're not going to end poverty, hunger, or homelessness through a single act of mercy, but we can offer temporary relief. For a moment we can become good news to someone in need of some good news.

As we discuss how to practically engage need in each context, it might be best to think of "mercy ministry" as anything that offers temporary relief to an immediate need. It's an immediate compassionate response of the heart. This might be a meal to the hungry, a coat for the homeless, or a visit to the widow. We're not going to end poverty, hunger, or homelessness through a single act of mercy, but we can offer temporary relief. For a moment we can become good news to someone in need of some good news.

While mercy ministry may offer temporary relief, "justice ministry" requires a greater level of personal investment. Justice typically focuses on both an increased awareness and an intentional and sustaining effort to confront a more global presence of need, such as the orphan crisis, human trafficking, or the need for clean water.

Both mercy and justice are motivated by compassion; each requires a physical response at different levels, and each benefits from increasing awareness. Both can exist independent of one another, yet together they encompass the biblical concept of serving the least. An act of mercy can quickly become an act of justice when a need is engaged through an intentional relationship. Mercy offers relief and compassion. Justice offers an advocate and action.

Simply put, mercy offers immediate and compassionate treatment of those in distress,[8] and justice is the principle or ideal of just dealing or right action.[9] Scripture clearly calls us to act justly and to love mercy (Micah 6:8). Hopefully we can quickly move beyond the questions of "who and why" and on to the realities of "what, when, and how."

CHAPTER 2

A Call and a Response

Recently, Austin New Church (ANC) partnered with a handful of Austin area nonprofits to increase awareness on the issue of human trafficking. Since we planned to show the documentary *Call and Response*, we got together prior to the event with our staff and spouses to preview the Justin Dillon film. Our hope was to process it together, get some feedback, and help inform any final preparations.

It's always great to mix together with our team, but our challenge is often the ability to drop the topics that seem to consume our common "church" workday and enjoy each other's company. Easier said than done. We talked about next week's service projects, about progress on the training for our new Restore Community leaders, as well as about some other typical church staff topics.

The film offered immediate perspective. My mind quickly shifted from our common church issues to images of twelve-year-old girls trapped in sex trafficking, women resorting to being mail-order brides with the hope of escaping poverty, and emotionless child soldiers walking around with AK-47s. It's amazing how an eighty-minute reminder of several massive issues in the world can shed light on how distracted we are from the things of true significance. There are an estimated twenty-seven million slaves in our world today. That's more than ever in history. Yet for the majority of the day my mind was consumed by trying to place a forty-something-year-old couple in community although they couldn't meet on days that ended in "y" or between the hours of 8:00 a.m. and 10:00 p.m.

After the film, in an unfair swing of emotions, I instantly felt indignation toward every Christian who had ever attended any church anywhere ... ever. Including myself. In a broken world in need of hope, it's depressing to consider the details that take priority in our minds. And it's embarrassing to think about the topics we reason away, choosing to remain blissfully ignorant while maintaining business as usual.

We are to love our neighbor as we do ourselves. Yet we think more about our Sunday bulletin than we think about the orphan crisis in our world. We believe the church is to be like a city on a hill and a light to the world, but we're more concerned about the new recessed lighting in our lobbies than we are poverty in our city.

As believers, we have got to find a way to see poverty and injustice in the world as wrong and worth fighting against.

I'm not convinced that we're really convinced.

Justin Dillon hit the nail on the head in the *Call and Response* documentary when he said, "If you truly love somebody, then you hate to see them treated unjustly."[1] I'm not convinced we even know what it means to love our neighbor. I'm not convinced we care. I'm not convinced because if we did, it would change the way we live.

As believers, we have got to find a way to see poverty and injustice in the world as wrong and worth fighting against. We need our neglect to be exposed. We need to see the indictment of Scripture. And we need to decide to no longer stand for it.

Richard Stearns, president and founder of World Vision, offers some bold direction on God's expectations for Christ followers: "Those expectations are not mysterious or difficult to discern. They are, in fact, etched clearly in page after page of Scripture—a bright thread of God's compassion for people and His zeal for justice."[2]

He has shown you, O mortal, what is good.
　And what does the LORD require of you?
To act justly and to love mercy
　and to walk humbly with your God.

MICAH 6:8

Matthew 25 gives a clear vision that when we serve the least we serve Jesus — that somehow and someway our eternity will be connected with how we respond to the least.

> They also will answer, "Lord, when did we see you hungry or thirsty or a stranger or needing clothes or sick or in prison, and did not help you?"
>
> He will reply, "Truly I tell you, whatever you did not do for one of the least of these, you did not do for me."
>
> Then they will go away to eternal punishment, but the righteous to eternal life.

MATTHEW 25:44 – 46

Stearns offers a modern-day version of this passage:

> For I was hungry, while you had all you needed. I was thirsty, but you drank bottled water. I was a stranger, and you wanted me deported. I needed clothes, but you needed more clothes. I was sick, and you pointed out the behaviors that led to my sickness. I was in prison, and you said I was getting what I deserved.

RESV — RICHARD E. STEARNS VERSION

If we were honest, our response to the poor might sometimes be better described by this irreverent version. Whatever the case, Christ's words in this passage cannot be dismissed out of hand. We have to face their implications no matter how disquieting. God has clear expectations for those who choose to follow Him. Any authentic and genuine commitment to Christ will be accompanied by demonstrable evidence of a transformed life. In contemporary terms, those who talk the talk but do not walk the walk will be exposed as false.[3]

We know that we have come to know him if we keep his commands. Whoever says, "I know him," but does not do what he commands is a liar, and the truth is not in that person.

1 JOHN 2:3 – 4

We feel bad. We recognize need. We talk about it with others, buy the T-shirt, and even read the books. But so often we fall short of doing anything. We often confuse the heart of compassion that requires a response with the feeling of sympathy that remains idle.

Most of us hear about need and sympathize. But that's not compassion. It's not justice. It's not mercy. Sympathy remains only sympathy until we do something about it. Then it becomes an act of compassion: an appropriate response to the call of need. Justin Dillon described it best: "A call is someone sharing their need. Sharing their oppression. A response is someone saying I hear you, I get you, and here's what I'm gonna do."[4]

I once read an anonymous quote that I think captures our situation well:

Sometimes I would like to ask God why He allows poverty, suffering, and injustice when He could do something about it. But, I'm afraid He would ask me the same question.

THERE IS HOPE FOR US

Misguided and shortsighted intentions are not new to Christianity. Time after time the disciples misunderstood the way and intent of Jesus. Yet there was hope. They often tried to sabotage his message and make it about themselves. Yet there was hope. They would have loved to just set up camp and stay with Jesus after the transfiguration (Luke 9:28 – 36). After seeing the humility of Jesus firsthand, they still argued over which one of them would be the greatest in the kingdom (Luke 9:46 – 48). It even came to the point where Jesus had to threaten to withhold eternity from them if they didn't change their ways (Matthew 18:3).

At times the disciples were self-centered. Yet there was hope. There is always hope, even in our neglect. When doing right becomes our plan, when that's our heart's motive and our desire, there is hope. And Scripture reveals that our hope will always start with love and faithfulness. It's through love and faithfulness that our neglect is overlooked. It's through realizing his kingdom, replacing our plans with his plans, that we succeed.

When doing right becomes our plan, when that's our heart's motive and our desire, there is hope.

> To humans belong the plans of the heart,
>> but from the LORD comes the proper answer of the tongue.
> All a person's ways seem pure to them,
>> but motives are weighed by the LORD.
> Commit to the LORD whatever you do,
>> and he will establish your plans....
> Through love and faithfulness sin is atoned for;
>> through the fear of the LORD evil is avoided.
> When the LORD takes pleasure in anyone's way,
>> he causes their enemies to make peace with them.
>> PROVERBS 16:1–3, 6–7

Peter, the one promised the keys to the kingdom, denied Jesus three times. Yet there was hope, and it started with the issue of love. In John 21:15, when Jesus reinstates Peter, he starts with a question: "Simon son of John, do you love me more than these?" This was a heart-wrenching question for Peter. First, Jesus calls him by the name he had prior to meeting Jesus, representing that he had taken a few steps back in his faith.

Second, Jesus challenges his love. This question could be translated in any one of three ways: (1) Do you love me more than these men love me? (2) Do you love me more than you love these men? (3) Do you love me more than you love your things? Each possibility proposes a unique question when thinking about our love of and loyalty to Jesus and our commitment to his way. Why do we live the way we live? Why do we do the things we do? Why do we not do what we do not do?

Is it possibly because we don't love Jesus enough? Is it because we love the opinion of others and value what they think over what Jesus values and what Jesus thinks? Is it because we love our stuff more than we love the things of Jesus? Each question is unique and expresses a different kind of love, yet each has the same antidote: love, concern, and sacrifice for others.

> "Yes, Lord," he said, "you know that I love you."
> Jesus said, "Feed my lambs."
> Again Jesus said, "Simon son of John, do you love me?"
> He answered, "Yes, Lord, you know that I love you."
> Jesus said, "Take care of my sheep."
> The third time he said to him, "Simon son of John, do you love me?"
> Peter was hurt because Jesus asked him the third time, "Do you love me?" He said, "Lord, you know all things; you know that I love you."
> Jesus said, "Feed my sheep."
>
> JOHN 21:15–17

The precedent for expressing love to Jesus was captured in three similar responses: "Feed my lambs." "Take care of my sheep." "Feed my sheep." Whether or not Jesus meant to "feed" them as a spiritual response or a physical calling, the end result will be the same. I'm not arguing that the sheep and lambs are to be direct representatives of orphans or the oppressed of the world. But it is worth noting that lambs and sheep have always come with a sense of ownership and value; they are labels of endearment and an expression of Jesus' concern for all.

What I am arguing is that Jesus was *not* talking about feeding ourselves. He was *not* talking about taking care of ourselves. We still do those things. But he wasn't saying to prove our love to him by keeping everything in house. Our hope is not found there. In fact, he was saying the exact opposite: the way to be reinstated, the way to change, the way to prove our love to him is to take care of others. Our hope lies in relearning our call to love our neighbor.

But who is our neighbor?

For so long, "loving our neighbors as ourselves" has meant loving our immediate neighbors, the ones who live next door. For the most part, it has been impossible to "love" people thousands of miles away. Only in the last century have we been able to have an awareness of their needs. It may have seemed ridiculous even to fathom that one's "neighbors" might include those living in another country. "For the general public, three major impediments stood in the way of anyone wanting to love their distant neighbors, even into the mid-twentieth century: awareness, access, and ability."[5]

The arrival of the communication age and technological advances have made the world a small place. I can pick up the phone right now and call my missionary friend in Addis Ababa, Ethiopia, and hear about needs in their community. I can literally be on the ground to help them by tomorrow. At the present time, every dollar I have is multiplied sixteenfold when exchanged into Ethiopian currency.

Awareness, access, and ability are no longer barriers even to the average Christian. They are no longer impediments in defining our neighbor. The gospel declares that everyone in need is our neighbor. In the story of the good Samaritan, Jesus asked the expert in the law which of the three was a "neighbor" to the man who fell into the hands of the robbers. His answer: "The one who had mercy on him."

Jesus did not define "neighbor" by proximity. He defined it by mercy.

Jesus' response: "Go and do likewise" (Luke 10:37).

Jesus did not define "neighbor" by proximity. He defined it by mercy. The whole world is our neighbor. Only after we move past the argument of who our neighbors are and what Jesus meant by loving them will we be moved to accomplish anything of significance. Until then, our questions remain excuses.

Jesus tells us clearly to "go and do likewise." Throughout Scripture we are reminded that our response will greatly impact how God responds to us. Our response will have everything to do with how God values the other things of faith that we value. Probably more than we realize:

God: "Do you want me to take pleasure in your worship?"
Us: "Yes."
God: "Seek justice."

God: "Do you want me to hear your prayers?"
Us: "Of course."
God: "Defend the cause of the fatherless."

God: "Do you want the sacrifices you make to matter to me?"
Us: "Sure. We've given up so much."
God: "Plead the case of the widow."

Do you really want to stop trampling my courts? Do you really want your fasting to be worship? Do you really want to hear "well done"? Do you really want to stop wasting all of your time? Do you really want to make disciples? Do you really care what I think?

> Learn to do right; seek justice.
> Defend the oppressed.
> Take up the cause of the fatherless;
> plead the case of the widow.
>
> ISAIAH 1:17

Herein lies our hope. Are you tired of ho-hum Christianity and powerless ministry? Do you really want your light to break forth and my kingdom to break through?

> *Then* your light will break forth like the dawn,
> and your healing will quickly appear;
> *then* your righteousness will go before you,
> and the glory of the LORD will be your rear guard.
> *Then* you will call, and the LORD will answer;
> you will cry for help, and he will say: Here am I.

If you do away with the yoke of oppression,
    with the pointing finger and malicious talk,
and if you spend yourselves in behalf of the hungry
    and satisfy the needs of the oppressed,
then your light will rise in the darkness,
    and your night will become like the noonday.
The LORD will guide you always;
    he will satisfy your needs in a sun-scorched land
    and will strengthen your frame.
You will be like a well-watered garden,
    like a spring whose waters never fail.

ISAIAH 58:8 – 11 (EMPHASIS ADDED)

PRAY FOR WISDOM

The book of James says that if we lack wisdom, we must pray for it (James 1:5). If in any way we need more prayer, it's for wisdom on how to engage need in our world. James basically spends the rest of his efforts explaining what wisdom looks like and why we need it: to actually do what the Bible says (James 1:22). *Pure religion* is a religion:

- that not only keeps itself unpolluted by the world, but literally spends itself on behalf of the orphan and widow (James 1:27).
- that sees loving our neighbor is the "royal law," and by keeping it we can eliminate any doubt as to what it means to do right (James 2:8).
- that lives out mercy triumphing over judgment (James 2:13).
- that sees faith without deeds as worthless (James 2:16, 20).
- that teaches knowledge is beneficial only when applied to a good life and humble deeds (James 3:13).
- that shows how wisdom resulting in selfish ambition is unspiritual, but wisdom from heaven is full of mercy and good fruit (James 3:15 – 17).

- that knows that when there is good to do, we sin when we fail to do it (James 4:17).
- that understands how our self-indulgence and our neglect have made us the oppressors (James 5:1 – 6).

If this is our condition, we're in trouble, and we certainly need wisdom.

> Is anyone among you in trouble? Let them pray ... And the prayer offered in faith will make the sick person well; the Lord will raise them up. If they have sinned, they will be forgiven. Therefore confess your sins to each other and pray for each other so that you may be healed.
>
> JAMES 5:13 – 16

If in anything we need more healing, it's in how we deal with needs in the world. If the statistics don't create a sense of indignation in us, then we should pray. If God's words do not create a sense of indignation for our condition, lack of concern, or neglect, we should pray that they do. Pray that the Holy Spirit convicts us. Pray that our minds are renewed. Pray for indignation. "Each individual has the spiritual responsibility of cultivating that indignation. Tapping into that rage. And then allowing that rage to be converted into compassionate action."[6]

It's both a personal and a collective responsibility. If no one else will go, we must still go. If no one else will care, we must still care. If every Christian in the world thinks we're crazy, it doesn't matter. In our indignation we will find joy, and the joy of the Lord is our strength (Nehemiah 8:10). We will find it to be our heart's delight. And in that joy we will find hope for both ourselves and for the church. For when we live recklessly by the Word and commands of God, we bear his name, not ours.

> When your words came, I ate them;
> > they were my joy and my heart's delight,
> for I bear your name,
> > LORD God Almighty.

I never sat in the company of revelers,
  never made merry with them;
I sat alone because your hand was on me
  and you had filled me with indignation.

JEREMIAH 15:16 – 17

INDIGNATION

In 2007 my friend Chris was invited to go on a trip to Zimbabwe to deliver some much-needed supplies to an orphanage they support. It was his first international trip and his first time seeing extreme poverty up close and personal. Since Zimbabwe was a "failed" state, lacking the most basic needs such as food, water, and fuel, the group had to purchase the supplies in South Africa and transport the goods in a gutted fifteen-passenger van. It was like liquid gold on wheels, loaded with food, water, and fuel.

As they drove down the dilapidated highway in the middle of the night, Chris recalled the overwhelming feeling of disbelief in seeing so many people living on the side of the road, hoping and waiting for relief. People were everywhere. Need was evident. Suffering was common.

They were driving with a local pastor, John, and his wife, Orpa. While there is little you can do to prepare emotionally for encountering extreme poverty for the first time, John had done his best to mentally prepare Chris for what he would experience. After a cultural crash course on the road, Chris was equipped with the bare minimum. A frequent experience around such levels of poverty is that everyone — literally everyone — will be asking for money or food. The company line: "I have nothing for you." It wasn't a lie. Even with a van packed with supplies, it would be true. The goods were designated for the thirty-five hungry orphans down the road.

Before making it to their final destination, John decided to make a quick stop in downtown Harare to check on some street kids he had begun to develop relationships with. As they drove into the abandoned gas station, hundreds of children swarmed their van.

Chris got out, and like a rock star, was immediately surrounded by curious bystanders.

Then it happened.

A dirty little hand tugged on his arm. He looked down to see a young boy staring back at him saying in broken English, "Sir, thank you for visit my country. I'm sorry it's in the state that it's in. I don't want to beg, but I'm hungry. I have no food in days. Is there any work I can do for you, so I can get some food?"

With both humility and hope in his eyes, he prepared himself for Chris's response.

"I'm sorry. I have nothing for you."

It was a simple and heartbreaking response, for both of them. In that twenty seconds, Chris's entire world changed.

They got back into the van — filled with food — and drove on to the orphanage. He sat there for the next forty minutes in silence while indignation filled his heart. In those forty minutes, he committed himself to a life where he would never have to say those words again.

Since then Chris has started the organization Help End Local Poverty (HELP), focused on serving orphans and fighting poverty. He has dedicated his life to spreading awareness through telling his story and empowering people to make a difference in tangible ways through a myriad of projects and ministries in Zimbabwe and Haiti.

It didn't start with a dream to begin a nonprofit. It started with seeing a need, hearing a call, and responding with compassion.

I love that Chris named his organization Help End Local Poverty. When we think of need globally, we often get stuck somewhere between ignorance and paralysis. While his story brought him across the ocean to encounter a boy who spoke in broken English, ours can start across the street, but only if we're willing to open our eyes and only if we're willing to go. There is hope for us, and we will find it when we follow the words of Jesus, "Go and do likewise."

"Let us touch the dying, the poor, the lonely and the unwanted according to the graces we have received and let us not be ashamed or slow to do the humble work." — Mother Teresa

CHAPTER 3

Where Gathering and Scattering Collide

Several years ago, I woke up around 4:00 a.m. with the feeling that someone was in my bedroom staring at me. It was a creepy feeling. Caught between the sluggish struggle of breaking out of REM sleep and the adrenaline rush of fear, my heart pounded as I opened my eyes.

I discovered that my five-year-old son had made his way into our room, wiggled his way under my covers, and was lying on my chest face-to-face with me with his nose about three inches from my nose. Before I could say a word, he blurted out,

"I want some chocolate milk."

"What?" I replied.

"I want some chocolate milk," he repeated.

Now, for the average five-year-old, this might not be a strange request. But at 4:00 a.m., it comes across as a bit presumptive and certainly as a premature way to launch the day. So I told him, "Go back to bed. It's not morning yet."

Closing my eyes, I hoped he'd get the hint and humbly and obediently obey my command. Yet he remained. Tapped me on the forehead. And repeated his request.

"I want some chocolate milk."

In my wisdom and maturity, I responded with some of the best words a father could offer. Parents take note in case you need to call upon this brilliance one day: "You want chocolate milk? I want a million dollars."

To which he wittily replied, "Well, I want five dollars ... for some chocolate and some milk."

Stunned by his mathematical accuracy, I got out of bed and whipped up some chocolate milk.

Chocolate and milk are two very different things, but as my son was well aware that morning—they taste great together. Each is fine on its own, but when you combine them you create something delicious, something worth getting out of bed to enjoy.

What does any of this have to do with the church? Well, when we first began to explore the reality of a socially active church, we observed a camp divided. We looked out at the landscape of the church world and saw two different patterns at work. Few churches were able to gather any attractional momentum while also engaging in the sacrifice of sending. In fact, most of the organizations that focused on the outward ministry were typically parachurch ministries or nonprofit organizations. While churches focused on attracting people and gathering them in, nonprofits and parachurch ministries were sending people out. The prevailing thought seemed to be: "Since you can't do both well, do one with excellence."

> I long to see a day when we look at the gathering and scattering of the church and value exaltation and incarnation *equally*.

But I'm not convinced this is true.

For anyone who equally values the gathering and the sending of the church, this divide creates a dilemma. While gathering and sending are indeed two different things, they seem more like chocolate and milk to me: two great things individually that work even better together. It's hard for us to imagine a day before chocolate milk existed. I long to see a day when we look at the gathering and scattering of the church and value exaltation and incarnation *equally*. It will be a day where it's hard to imagine them operating separately and impossible to evaluate success independently, and their value will be inextricably linked.

HURRICANE IKE

In September 2008, Austin was abuzz with rumors about the path of Hurricane Ike making its way into the Gulf of Mexico with an eye on the Texas coast. This was a huge concern for the people of Austin because we quickly became the home to thousands of refugees in need.

Although Ike made its final landfall near Galveston, Texas, as only a Category 2 hurricane, it packed a powerful punch with the equivalent storm surge of a Category 5. This was bad news for many people. And the flood of refugees reaching Austin filled our shelters in a matter of hours.

That afternoon, I received a call from the Austin Baptist Association, which informed me they had a Spanish-speaking family at the office in need. The father was a pastor from an east Houston suburb who had nowhere to go and was asking for help. With such young children, they could not go to the shelters. They had no money for a hotel, and they had contacted all of the Spanish-speaking churches in the area to no avail.

So they asked if we could help. I called Jen, and without hesitation, we decided to accept their family into our home. That was the day I was educated on how "family" can mean two different things between cultures. Within twenty-four hours, we had eighty-two of their "family" at our house.

It was the best thing that ever happened to our young church.

Instantly, our church became "the church." Without prompting, people from ANC and the community began to call and email to offer their homes as refuge. People cleaned out Wal-Mart of sleeping bags and dropped them off. Food was everywhere, grill-outs were planned, events for the kids fell into place ... honestly, it was beautiful.

And it was fun. Not once did I feel personally put out. Not once that week did anyone complain about their plans being canceled to serve those in need. No one sent an email about Bible study not being "deep" enough. No one worried about the children's ministry sign-in process. No one complained that they had to give money to help. They just gave. All they could. They gave without coercion or guilt. Smiles everywhere. Joy everywhere.

In a world where we are constantly asking what went wrong, I couldn't help but ask, What went right?

The next Sunday's worship gathering was simply amazing. Everyone, literally everyone, who was a part of ANC was in attendance. The Spirit was thick. The worship was pure. The sharing was raw. Everyone was thankful for what they had and thankful to be able to give. Undoubtedly, it was the most intuitively worshipful gathering we had ever had.

In a world where we are constantly asking what went wrong, I couldn't help but ask: What went right? What made that day so sweet? I think the answer lies in what Scripture tells us makes our worship meaningless. This is at the heart of Isaiah 1 and is a huge accusation toward the nation of Israel:

> "The multitude of your sacrifices —
>   what are they to me?" says the LORD.
> "I have more than enough of burnt offerings,
>   of rams and the fat of fattened animals;
> I have no pleasure
>   in the blood of bulls and lambs and goats.
> When you come to appear before me,
>   who has asked this of you,
>   this trampling of my courts?
> Stop bringing meaningless offerings!
>   Your incense is detestable to me...
>   I cannot bear your worthless assemblies.
> Your New Moon feasts and your appointed festivals
>   I hate with all my being.

They have become a burden to me;
    I am weary of bearing them.
When you spread out your hands in prayer,
    I hide my eyes from you;
even when you offer many prayers,
    I am not listening."

ISAIAH 1:11–15

The prophet Isaiah lets us know that God was ticked off. He's made that crystal clear. He let the nation of Israel know that for some reason, he no longer took pleasure in their worship. Not only did he take no pleasure in it, he says that it had become a burden to him. He was even weary of it.

If God finds no pleasure in our worship, yet we continue to worship, then who is it for? The answer is easy. It's for us. When that happens, according to Isaiah, God considers even our worship evil. Seems pretty counterproductive to me. And he goes beyond that. Because of this, he won't even listen to our prayers, even if we pray a lot. He's so serious about this that Scripture says he doesn't even want to look at us.

It wasn't their style or method of worship that was making God angry. They were worshiping with the precision in which they were instructed. What he was saying is that something had taken place that was inhibiting their worship from achieving its goal. That there was something else going on that had defiled a pure thing.

Recently, I found out that a close friend felt differently about something than what he had represented to me. To me he agreed, but in different company, he opposed. It was something very personal, so his double standard was hurtful. As much as I wanted just to decide it wasn't that big of a deal, it was a big deal. Every word he said seemed to lack sincerity and integrity. It literally got to the point where I didn't want to be around him. Knowing what I knew, it seemed antagonistic and condescending that he would even talk to me.

Is it possible that this is what was happening in Isaiah 1? Is this how God feels when we worship him and yet ignore other aspects of living sent lives? Is it antagonistic? Are we standing in ignorance, thinking he doesn't know what we do or don't do? Could our neglect keep him from wanting to hear our prayers or even see our face?

Isaiah 1 says yes. There's something big they neglected—and it changed everything. Here was God's instruction on how to make it right:

> Wash and make yourselves clean.
>> Take your evil deeds out of my sight;
>> stop doing wrong.
> Learn to do right; seek justice.
>> Defend the oppressed.
> Take up the cause of the fatherless;
>> plead the case of the widow.
>
> ISAIAH 1:16–17

God couldn't have made this clearer. Throughout Scripture, he reminds Israel that his greatest indictment is their neglect of the poor and oppressed. And it's not just worship that's impacted. While Isaiah reminds us that serving the poor validates our worship (Isaiah 1) and fasting (Isaiah 58), James reminds us that it gives evidence of our faith (James 4), and Jesus reminds us that it is somehow linked to our eternity (Matthew 25).

We were in the middle of a season of prayer for wisdom on how the gathering and the sending biblically collided when we encountered Hurricane Ike. Ironically and specifically, we were wondering if gathering and sending could structurally coexist effectively. What Scripture tells us is that somehow, biblically, they must. And if we value them as God values them, we'll see that they actually strengthen one another.

The truth is, when we give away our resources, we can't do as much with the gathering—especially when it costs money to serve the poor. On the flip side, when we spend it on the weekend, we don't have it to give away. That's our dilemma. To some it's a crisis, especially organizationally. Can we ever have our cake and eat it, too? Many say no ... so we choose one as a priority and give to the other whatever's left. It's easier to choose one or the other, yet Scripture never releases us from either.

Our journey is not about finding a place where we no longer have to struggle to balance this. According to the Bible, the goal is not to live without the struggle; the goal is to find God and deny ourselves throughout the struggle.

According to the Bible, the goal is not to live without the struggle; the goal is to find God and deny ourselves throughout the struggle.

DO WE SEE THE CRISIS?

Hurricane Ike taught us that in times of crisis, the church most intuitively becomes the church. Since the simple fruit of crisis is need, they go hand in hand. This makes much sense of why Jesus would give us the example of engaging need as a first step to being missionaries to our culture. When we engage need individually and as a body, we most closely resemble Christ.

Our problem is most exposed when we do not see the need.

I've always been enamored with the rapid growth of the early church, and I've been similarly captivated by the rapid growth of the modern church in places like China. The common denominator is persecution. The crisis is obvious. They are in need, and all the believers involved intuitively know it. The result? The church is more vibrant, it's more engaged, and it's more desperate. It's more in need of God's leading, God's blessing, God's provision. Thus, they hunger and thirst for God's righteousness.

Because of our plenty, we don't see need in America as we see it in other places where God seems to be moving mightily. Not tangible, critical, life-altering need. It's mostly need that can be hidden or ignored. It's mostly need that we can suppress while continuing to do our outwardly religious activities. Our problem is most exposed when we do not see the need.

But there is crisis in America. There's a void of Spirit. There's a lack of powerful transformation. And studies show that people are leaving the church. Scripture says that we're to be a city on a hill that cannot be hidden. Like it or not, that's not the reputation of the Western church. Not only are we hidden in our culture as something that is supposed to be good news, we're losing ground.

Things changed for ANC after Hurricane Ike because we began to do the most natural thing when it came to meeting needs during a crisis. We began to see the various forms of need in our community as different kinds of crisis in our community — and we began to realize the church's responsibility to engage them all. When we do, it makes the gathering all that much better.

In response, we began to develop a structure and process to expose, experience, and engage need as a funnel for spiritual formation. Every need, whether it is a physical need for food or a spiritual need for food, must be *exposed* and *seen*. That's the responsibility of every spiritual leader. Need is everywhere, yet somehow we have conditioned our eyes not to see it. We see problems. We see things to avoid. We see things that aren't right; but when we don't see them as needs, we're less likely to realize we are the ones who should do something about it.

If you're anything like me, you probably don't know where to start. Neither do most people. If we are tasked as the church to equip people for ministry, the obvious next step is to help them *experience* it in some kind of simple environment. Maybe it's a project. Maybe it's an event. Whatever it is, its design is to simply taste and see. Once we experience need, our gifting, experiences, and passion seem to intuitively draw us deeper into the areas where we are best equipped or called to serve.

From there, we must do our best to *engage* the need personally. We believe the best way to do that is through community. When we serve in relationship with others, we are much more likely to engage need as a part of our normal life rhythms — and vice versa.

Exposing Need

Any church that gathers has an opportunity on Sunday to hold the attention of the entire church family. We come together to worship, to teach, and to take communion. We encourage and we lead. We equip and we exhort, all in just one hour a week. That's a tough task. But if ever there is an opportunity to expose need in our community and world, it's then.

With this in mind, we've chosen to teach through Scripture on Sundays and let the topics be chosen by the text. It's not that we think that's the only way to teach during a worship gathering; we just believe it's a great way to keep focus completely vertical between the people and God. If our focus of a Sunday gathering is exaltation and adoration, we hope to do everything we can to point people toward a vertical focus.

You will find, as we have, that Scripture exposes need with every verse. Spiritual need? Check. Relational need? Check. Physical need? Check. It's not a stretch to apply Scripture directly to mission. And we're never at a loss for seeing what we can and should do next. Combine that with some creative promotional efforts and intentional partnerships, and we'll be exposing need at levels few of us have ever seen. We're not creating need; we're exposing the need that is all around us. We're training our people to see with new eyes. It's a bit embarrassing when we realize how long we've been surrounded by need, and yet have walked blindly through it. We can't help but want to respond. People will be motivated to do something significant—with purpose and with a hope to be good news.

> You will find, as we have, that Scripture exposes need with every verse.

Experiencing Need

Even if we expose need and people want to do something about it, there is still no guarantee they will do anything new. This is the stopping point for many of us. We leave a gathering all pumped up ready to do something, and then real life hits. Good intentions can often remain just that. I'm sure you can relate. Deadlines are approaching, bills have to be paid, and school projects that require your help are waiting on the kitchen countertop.

In other words, without a trans- formed heart, we simply won't want to serve.

We have some deeper issues, too. Beyond being selfish, unmotivated, and unconvinced, the big issue is that our flesh literally opposes it. In other words, without a transformed heart, we simply won't want to serve. While it's an ugly truth, it's good to be honest with ourselves and know our starting point. Paul wrote in Galatians 5:17, "For the flesh desires what is contrary to the Spirit, and the Spirit what is contrary to the flesh. They are in conflict with each other, so that you are not to do whatever you want."

We feel sympathy for those in need. But it's the Spirit that leads us to compassion. And there is a huge difference between the two. We can't make ourselves change the way we feel. But we can change what we do and trust that the Spirit will move. Richard Rohr, author of *Simplicity*, put it this way, "You cannot think your way into a new way of living. You have to live your way into a new way of thinking."[1]

The Spirit is moving. When we act, the Spirit moves in us. So how should we act? What should we do? I recall being told to go out there and be a "light." I'd leave church all excited and feeling like, "Alright here we go, be a light … uh … bright and shining … uh … what does that really mean?"

It's the same way with serving. We tell people to serve. Or maybe we're the ones told to serve, and we may even really want to, but our willpower is small, almost as small as our insight on where to start.

I remember tasking a group to go find a project in their area where they could serve. A month later, I asked the leader how it was going. His reply? He had sent an email a month previous and hadn't heard anything back yet. Okay, I thought, send another email then. Brilliant! Another email.

One month later I saw the same leader. "How's the project going? Did you land on something?"

"I never heard back from the second email. I don't know what's wrong with them."

I know this sounds harsh, but sometimes we play dumb and we don't even know it. Seriously. In our careers, we have to be problem solvers. We run into an issue and we find a solution, or they'll hire someone else to find a solution. So here was my next solution: "Do you have a phone? Try that."

Four months into the process, two emails and a phone call later, this highly skilled leader found out that the event for which they wanted to volunteer had already taken place a week earlier. And for some reason, they felt as if it was someone else's fault that they didn't have a project to do.

We've got to own this a little more. We need to take initiative. But as a church leader, I can't assume someone is going to do that. As much as I want them to "help me help you," often they don't. So we created an opportunity where people can start by taking part in a service day where they can taste what it's all about.

I know it sounds weird to taste need, but that's what it is: an event designed for people just to show up and feel what it's like to serve. It's a critical step. Ours comes in the form of an event we call Serve Austin Sunday (SAS). On fifth Sundays, our church cancels our regular worship gathering to go *be* the church. We choose a number of projects to do with strategic nonprofit organizations across our city and just go out and serve together.

Although this event is designed as an entry-level service opportunity, it's amazing how much it impacts those who've never served. It's amazing to see how easy it is to invite a neighbor to join us. And it's amazing to see how quickly people grow when they step into leading at the event itself rather than simply attending. For some, it's a culture shock such as they've never experienced before. It's incredible how many people have never done anything for someone in need.

There are three reasons we do this on a Sunday in lieu of our normal worship gatherings.

It creates a service-minded DNA. We want to make sure we communicate serving the least as a priority to our church. This has worked great in that we typically have more people show up for this project than we do a normal worship service. That's rare!

In fact, it's working so well that we now have a network of churches joining us for Serve Austin Sundays. Recently, we had a small church join us that expected to have 30 people show up out of their typical 110. To their surprise, they had 130 people show up. If we were to simply add serving to our regularly scheduled Sunday gathering, I would imagine attendance would drop at least 50 percent, but probably more like 80 percent. In fact, that's exactly what we've found. The churches that join us to serve Sunday afternoon in addition to their Sunday morning services have a significantly lower percentage of people involved. If we're trying to create a culture of service, we have to communicate and structure serving as a priority, not as an add-on or optional event.

It changes our posture to the community. One of the most surprising and unexpected benefits of collectively serving on Sunday is what it communicates to the skeptics of our community. What they see is that we value worship, but just as important is that we are a church that attempts to match our deed with our creed. When speaking of what we do for Serve Austin Sunday to those outside the church, they are curious about the "what" and "why" of our projects, but they are dumbfounded that we actually cancel our normal Sunday services to do it. This goes a long way in changing people's perceptions of church in our community.

The opportunity to invite others. Serve Austin Sunday is hands down our most highly attended Sunday by nonbelievers, skeptics, the unchurched, and the dechurched. It's easy to invite someone to join you to go downtown and grill burgers for homeless people or to go to a poor eastside elementary school to do a classroom makeover. It's much easier than dealing with the baggage that accompanies inviting someone to a church service—especially if they don't believe or understand the whole church thing anyway. People get service. They want to be a part of something significant. I'm constantly amazed by who might show up at a service project.

We used to do this event once a month. While that communicated a huge priority to service, we found that this was a good starting point, but not a good long-range plan. We had to find a way to help people engage need on a more personal level.

Engaging Need

As great as holding Serve Austin Sundays every month was, as our only service experience, it came with some inherent issues. Churchwide service projects are typically planned by church staff. They require staff to recruit the leaders, staff energy for promoting the event to get people there, and then the church typically pays for it. Honestly, that's an inhibitor to reproducibility because it requires drawing from a limited pool of resources and people. That's okay for a season of observation, but if we take spiritual formation seriously, eventually we need to get people to engage need on their own. It has to be decentralized.

With this in mind, we quickly and prayerfully decided that an "experience need" type of service event, while necessary, might be best utilized as a less frequently planned event. We wanted to help people engage need more personally and on a regular basis rather than at a monthly event they could just consume. That's where our Restore Communities came into play. The moment we charged our communities to serve once a month and moved Serve Austin Sundays to a once-per-quarter event, our church went from doing just one project to anywhere from twelve to twenty-five service projects a month. Through their own community groups, people planned, led, and served. Everything was taken care of in and through community. Service intuitively went from a potentially consumer experience to something lived out as a part of missional incarnational community.

> **We wanted to help people engage need more personally and on a regular basis rather than at a monthly event they could just consume.**

55

Hurricane Ike taught us to recognize crisis as need and that need is everywhere. We found that when we engage need as the church, we naturally become good news. When we're good news, it changes everything, including everything about our gathering.

Bill Cosby once said, "I don't know the secret to success, but the secret to failure is to try to please everybody." This might be our problem. We see focusing on gathering and sending as opposing things because it typically pleases two different types of people and serves two different functions. And it's true: it's hard to place our affections on sending people, resources, and attention outward when we're so in love with what we do inside the camp.

We need to come to grips with the reality that we're not here to please or impress each other and do only what we like or prefer. We're here to please God. We may have a calling, a gifting, or a leaning toward gathering or serving, but only by doing both do we become all things to all people. The apostle Paul put it this way, "As it is, there are many parts, but one body" (1 Corinthians 12:20).

CHAPTER 4

Serving through Missional Community

A couple of years ago, my wife, Jen, and I took a cruise from Seattle to Alaska for our anniversary. It was awesome. We had never been to Seattle, so we decided to fly in a few days early to take in the city. We did all the usual stops. We stood on the observation deck of the Space Needle, Jen caught a fish at Pike's Place Market, and since we're both huge coffee lovers, we figured we'd better check out the original Starbucks while we were there.

I was pretty pumped about the Starbucks thing. The line was out the door. The storefront was just like the pictures. And they were funneling people through as efficiently as possible, everyone leaving with their coffee and an additional T-shirt, mug, or other logo-laden paraphernalia. It was a whirlwind of action. I grabbed my black coffee and went to find a place to sit down while waiting for Jen and her eight-syllable drink when it hit me . . . *there are no chairs in this room.*

Surely not, this is Starbucks, home of community and wi-fi. The place we hang out for business meetings and stale pastries. Honestly, it set me back a moment. But they had removed every chair in the building to make room for in-and-out traffic. Tables too. What once was a place built on the idea of community had now become a business so efficient that no one in the room even noticed they were being herded around like cattle.

And we didn't care. They were giving us exactly what we wanted: coffee, a T-shirt, and a picture in front of the building to prove we had been there. No one was there to hang out, read a book, or sip on a latte. They had a tourist schedule and needed to move on.

This is church without missional community. Something built on relationships and unified effort, now a place to consume with a revolving door, a weekly tourist stop for the self-righteous. A place to get our fix and say we were there.

Every time I hear someone teach on the Acts 2 church I wonder what first-century faith community really looked like. I can't help but think there was something special about it that we've missed. It's hard to imagine a day where people would pool what they had to make sure no one was without. While things certainly look different in our time, it just seems as if we've lost a little something. Something tells me community didn't just fill a need in their lives to connect, it gave them purpose.

> **We never get to the bottom of our selves on our own. We discover who we are side by side with others in work, love, and learning.**

Robert Bellah, American sociologist and professor of sociology at the University of California in Berkeley, wrote: "We find ourselves not independently of other people and institutions but through them. We never get to the bottom of our selves on our own. We discover who we are side by side with others in work, love, and learning. All of our activity goes on in relationships, groups, associations, and communities ordered by institutional structures and interpreted by cultural patterns of meaning."[1]

In other words, we need each other. We were created that way. Whether we choose to be so or not, we are shaped by our relationships. We will be influenced and find our significance as believers in community. Jesus said that he had come to give life, and life to the full (John 10:10). Paul was clear in Ephesians that we were to "lead a life worthy of the calling" and to "make every effort" to live in unity (Ephesians 4:1, 3). It's through doing life together that we learn to do so. "The church is God's people gathered as a unit, as a people, gathered to do business in His name, to find what it means here and now to put into practice this different quality of life which is God's promise to them and to the world and their promise to God and service to the world."[2]

In learning to become a community that is "not about us," we more intuitively lean into the leading of the Spirit as we seek to participate in God's mission in the world. When we do so, it becomes a reminder of God's redemption, a preview of what that redemption is like, and it offers a strategy to carry redemption's hope into every context.[3]

In essence, missional community may serve as one of the best ways we can embody the incarnation of Christ — putting on flesh and being Jesus to our world. When we live this out, the focus of the church shifts to hearing and responding to the Spirit. When this is translated collectively, congregations as a whole tend to take more seriously the how and when to engage communities where they live.[4]

THE PROBLEM

Jen and I have our kids' school lunch account set up in such a way that when it gets below ten dollars, it automatically drafts from our checking account. This is designed to be a good thing. Last week, I was reconciling our checking account when I noticed an unusual amount of money being debited from the company who manages the lunch accounts. In fact, as I added them up for all three kids, it totaled $380 over the last thirty days.

After some investigation, I found that my seven-year-old had managed to forgo his standard, healthy, and low-priced school lunch, in his own words, to "upgrade" to three or four ice cream sandwiches every Wednesday and Friday. When I asked him why he would do that, he simply replied, "Because, Dad, they only serve ice cream on Wednesday and Friday."

Welcome to my world.

Although the money given was designated for healthy food, my son had chosen an unhealthy substitute that cost even more. This was a problem — and he was completely oblivious to it. So at the moment of purchase we're trying to get him to ask the question: Is what I'm about to do with this money in line with my parent's will and purpose for this money?

Just as church without community falls short of biblical church, Just as church without community falls short of biblical church, community without mission falls short of biblical community. I just can't help but ask the question: Is our typical idea of community in line with God's will and purpose for community?

community without mission falls short of biblical community. Most pastors I know would answer no. Many aren't content with the sense of community and mission in their church. If we were to take a hard look, we might not like what we see either. Yet our church is exactly where we've led it. That doesn't make us bad people or even bad leaders; it just means we may need to make some changes. Maybe it's time to take a hard look at our structure and see if it's fostering community that is growing out of culture or from the church down the street. We need to look at how we've organized ourselves and evaluate if we're making disciples on mission or fostering consumerism. More often than not, this has less to do with what we do on Sunday and everything to do with what we do Monday through Saturday. Our problem is most often what we think of when we envision "community."

OUR DILEMMA

While we started ANC with the homeless, a grill, and a prayer, the more we began to serve, the more we grew. Eventually we had people who needed to be led and who were looking for next steps. I sensed an inevitable road toward a worship gathering on Sunday. That scared me — not because I was against gathering on Sundays, but because I knew how quickly it can become *the* focus of a church, even for a church built on mission.

George Barna, in his recent book *Revolution,* concludes that by the year 2025 the spiritual profile of the nation will be dramatically different. Specifically, Barna expects that only about one-third of the population will rely on a local congregation as the primary or exclusive means for experiencing and expressing their faith; one-third will do so through alternative forms of faith-based community; and one-third will realize their faith through the media, the arts, and other cultural institutions.[5]

Essentially, he's saying that the church, as we know it, is dying. Dwindling at best. While I don't necessarily agree with the time line, what it tells me is that there's still time. There's a lot of ministry to be done with what we have between now and 2025. So what happens between now and 2025? The question kept coming to my mind: If the gathering church did disappear, if Sunday as we knew it went away, what would sustain us as a faith community? Do we have the community structures in place to survive the loss of our Sunday gatherings?

So we asked the question. In fact, for us, this became an excellent measuring stick for our ministry efforts and connectivity outside of Sunday. If the gathering disappeared, what would remain? And the collateral questions: What would happen to the mission? What would happen to community? What would happen to our incarnational efforts? What would happen to our church?

Answering these questions offers us some clear insight into how much our forms depend on us and our ability to empower our people to lead out in the community.

While I have no plans to end our weekly gathering for worship, I couldn't help but wonder if our service-oriented DNA was ingrained enough to keep it going without a weekly pep rally and

As long as serving remains an event that people attend, it never becomes self-sustaining, much less heart-transforming, regardless of how we change our weekend structure.

monthly service project. In answering these questions, I realized that serving for us was still an "event" and not as much a part of "going" as I knew it needed to be. We were not empowering our people enough, and our "form" was incomplete. As long as it was the pastors who planned, scheduled, promoted, and recruited for a service project, it would always just be something that had "attenders" and "volunteers." It would always be an event that could be consumed. As long as serving remains an event that people attend, it never becomes self-sustaining, much less heart-transforming, regardless of how we change our weekend structure.

CONFRONTING CONSUMERISM

As I mentioned earlier, up to this point in the history of our church, every service project we did was planned by our staff. We recruited the leaders for it. We promoted it. Our church paid for it. We tried to get people to show up to "our" event. And some did. But the very thing we had found to be a catalyst for transformation, getting people to take ownership for the mission, was lacking.

While most of our monthly service events were pretty good, we weren't structured to create a life of mission. As consumers ourselves, we had unknowingly built a paradigm that allowed our people to consume opportunities of service. Structurally, we were falling far short of our dream.

In our current structure, we found that we could pull off about one service project per month. By scheduling these on Sundays in lieu of a church gathering (and yes, no offering), we were certainly sending the message that service to our community was a priority. But, honestly, just planning one a month was wearing our staff and key leaders out. While literally everyone attended the project, it was always the same people leading it, and we were falling desperately short of making "serving the least" more than just another event. So we decided to make another change.

STRUCTURING TO SERVE

Instead of investing staff time planning these monthly church-wide events, we put the responsibility into the hands of our community groups. We changed the name of our Community Groups to "Restore Communities" with a new commitment to focus on "individual, collective, and social renewal." For eight weeks, we put our existing community groups on hold and trained our leaders for mission. We shaped our partner (membership) process to be a journey toward understanding and developing a missional theology. This included an eight-week course on creating incarnational community.

We found Hugh Halter and Matt Smay's resource, *The Tangible Kingdom Primer*,[6] to be a perfect fit for this equipping and have integrated it as a key element of our church's spiritual formation and partner process. Our goal in supporting our vision was to reevaluate who was really a part of our church community and to empower our leaders while relaunching our groups to engage need with a new structure. We were training them to not only serve the least, but our neighbors as well.

To do this, we recruited three groups of leaders for each community. The beauty of this approach is that each group instantly had six bought-in leaders who were committed to the mission and DNA of their group. One couple (the "hosts") was in charge of "hospitality" and coordinated communications, location for the meeting, the snacks, and the childcare. One couple (the "facilitators") was in charge of leading the Bible study, discussion, and prayer. And one couple (the "restore leaders") was in charge of "mission."

The "restore leaders" were responsible for making sure their group committed at least two of their community gatherings a month, half of their time, to either loving their neighbor or serving their city. The other half could be spent on them. That was it. Simple, really. If we love our neighbor as much as ourselves, why wouldn't we give away as much time as we keep?

So every other week we had dinner together, held a Bible study or spiritual discussion, and broke out into prayer groups. And on alternate weeks, we canceled the gathering to "Love Our Neighbor" by inviting a neighbor to dinner, throwing a party, planning a neighborhood family night, or some other strategically intentional effort to foster relationships; or we would "Serve Our City" by doing a family-friendly service project with one of our nonprofit partners in our city. Our mantra emerged: "Love your neighbor. Serve your city."

Our goal was *not* to control the process; it was to enable, encourage, and release our people for mission.

Since from the beginning we had made it a priority to have a pastor on staff whose primary responsibility was to develop partnerships with local nonprofits in our city, we already had a plug-and-play process for each restore leader to get their Restore Community connected with the project of their choice. We even gave them permission to find their own project if they wanted to. Our goal was *not* to control the process; it was to enable, encourage, and release our people for mission. Once the group had landed on a service opportunity, they signed themselves up, organized it, and paid for it. They did everything. Why? It was *their* project.

Along the way we were able to identify four critical leadership shifts that were required to empower our Restore Communities to serve. These changes required shifts ...

1. From Control to Accountability

One of the most difficult places to "let go" in ministry is with our community groups. The further away our ministries get from Sunday, the more high-risk they are. Often we're so afraid they'll go rogue that our leadership becomes suffocating. We need to be careful to check in and to check up, but not control the situation. When we control something, our people will never take ownership of it. Why would they if we are there to do it for them?

2. From Suspicion to Permission

It's critical that we clearly communicate in advance what the *goal* of missional community is and then give people permission to make it their own. Often we fall into the trap of trying to justify something by determining if it really benefits the organization. If our community is pointed outward by design, we don't have to wonder anymore. If they'e pursuing something worthwhile that serves our community with any sense of urgency at all, we should simply be glad they're out there doing it.

3. From Fixed to Flexible

Give it some time and let it get messy. A common mistake we make as leaders is rescuing a group too early. In community, finding solutions to problems or even navigating failure can be as effective as succeeding. That's what growth as a community is all about — learning from our mistakes together. We always offer suggestions with how and where to serve, but this is not to be inflexible; it's to make it easy for leaders to lead at the beginning. If the group has their own idea, as long as it's an idea of serving, they have the freedom to do so. Ultimately, the goal is to have a community take ownership of their projects.

4. From Majority to Priority

We really don't all have to be in the same boat. We can actually cover more ground in a bunch of medium-sized boats. But all of us do need to be rowing in the same direction with the same objective. The beauty is not found in the magnitude of the mission but in the priority it takes in our lives. We have to create structure and give permission to make mission and community a priority.

We always start with a structure to help create a group rhythm. As time passes they have the freedom to find their own schedule and to follow paths that might be more intuitive based on the makeup of their group. As mentioned before, when we launched this new initiative, we instantly went from one church-wide project a month to anywhere between twelve and twenty-four service projects a month, and the number of people involved in missional community literally quadrupled. Both have scaled accordingly as we've grown. Most of the projects were self-funded as well. What we found was that when it was a *structural necessity* for our people to be serving in the community, it automatically became an essential part of their spiritual formation. Best of all, our people were on mission *together*, and almost always this translated into a more personally engaged commitment to the work and the relationships.

Although we had been serving regularly as a church body from the launch of the church, serving through community in this way *literally* changed who we were as a church.

Although we had been serving regularly as a church body from the launch of the church, serving through community in this way *literally changed who we were as a church*. We found an experience of community such as we had never experienced before in weekly small groups. Since then, we've learned that when we seek community, we may or may not end up finding it. But whenever we lock our arms together for the sake of mission, we inevitably find community with those we serve with.

I know that can sound a bit strange, but just stop and think about it for a moment. Have you ever gone on a mission trip where you didn't come back feeling closer and more connected to the people you went with than you had before? There always seems to be a supernatural connection that forms when we serve alongside others, a connection that bridges our differences with one another. And that's what we found. We have missional communities that are geographical and some that are affinity based, but as we've served together, our church has emerged as a church that is as diverse as the city we serve.

REPRODUCING COMMUNITY

After several years of leading small groups, I've made a handful of observations. First of all, you can't force a group to be great. There is either a natural connection among the people in a group or there isn't. This is one of the reasons we don't funnel people into a community directly from our Sunday morning gatherings. Instead, we found it much more productive to train leaders and then try to send them out to start new groups with people they already know who don't attend a church. This is certainly a much slower process, but we've found that it always makes for better community.

Second, every small group has a certain shelf life. Most of the time that's because everyone eventually gets bored with the same-old-same-old. A community on mission together will typically maintain a longer life span as they work together to engage changing needs in the community.

And third, I've rarely seen a group that has successfully split down the middle to form two groups. One of the two groups always seems to dwindle or fade within a short period of time after the split.

> **Living on mission together for a period of time will inevitably create secondary relationships within a community that can easily become the primary focus.**

With this in mind, we must *create* a sending culture among our missional communities. If we don't do this, they'll eventually become lifeless social gatherings. This is nothing new. The early church leaders found ways to release their people for mission. They understood the critical connection between the success of the church's mission and their own willingness to empower others into significant leadership roles. "A failure to do this would have doomed the movement to be swamped by its early success"[7]

Living on mission together for a period of time will inevitably create secondary relationships within a community that can easily become the primary focus. Our strategy for multiplication is not splitting up groups; it's sending leaders out to start new groups that are formed out of their new relationships. We give each group the freedom to take on their own personality, and depending on the makeup of their group, a leader can shape it accordingly. In the two years since we've adopted this model, we've seen groups *multiply up to four times*. Each multiplication includes some of the people who were a part of the original group, but each is primarily made up of people from newly formed relationships that develop when serving outside of the church.

As with any church, every week we have people who show up at a Sunday gathering for the first time. Since it's a partner (membership) requirement and a key element of our spiritual formation process for people who attend to be in some type of community, they are quickly encouraged to get connected. But unless they already have a relational connection with a community, we try to avoid placing new people in existing groups. If we were to place them in an existing community group, we would instantly isolate that person from their current relationships and reduce their missionary potential. That's certainly not our goal!

Instead, we hold pilot groups, where we take these potential leaders through our training and encourage them to start a new group. Sometimes new communities form out of new relationships in the pilot group as we train these new leaders. Sometimes groups start out of existing relationships people already have outside of the church. Everyone knows someone. And most of those someones don't have a community of faith that they call home.

> The purpose of missional community is not to create a place where Christians can casually connect.

We require a lot from our Restore Communities. Since they are the place where we most hope to see individual, collective, and social renewal, we should expect a lot from them. After all, the purpose of missional community is not to create a place where Christians can casually connect. It's not just another place where we can study the Bible. It's not just a support group to help us cope with struggles.

The purpose of missional communities is to be a source of radical hope, to witness to the new identity and vision, the new way of life that has become a social reality in Jesus Christ through the power of the Holy Spirit. The persistent problem is not how to keep the church from withdrawing from the world, but how to keep the world from withdrawing from the church ... The forming of Christian community is therefore not an option but the very lifestyle and vocation of the church.[8]

CHAPTER 5

Good News for the Unchurched and Dechurched

Skeptics of church are just that—they're skeptics. And they don't believe what we believe or share our values. There is plenty of reason for that. In the advancing age of media, communications, and technology, any sign of corruption in the church can be worldwide within minutes. And what do they see? Leaders of major Christian organizations taking the fall on the very issue they've spoken out against for years, pastors living posh lives equivalent to Fortune 500 CEOs, and Koran burnings by hyperconservative Christian activists. I know this is an overgeneralization. But the whole church is taking a hit for the mistakes of a few of its leaders.

Recently Jerry Jones, the owner of the Dallas Cowboys, built a 1.3 billion dollar facility to house their 100,000 fans. The facility is the epitome of excessiveness. According to ESPN columnist Matt Mosley, Jerry's hope is that this stadium will be his family's legacy, even more so than his three Super Bowl rings.[1] Everything he has and hopes to be known for is encompassed by a building.

Just down the road from his $16K-per-seat dome sits the home of a church in the middle of a 130 million dollar building campaign. They're outdoing the famous tycoon by a whopping $27K per seat— at a total expected cost of $43K per seat.

While touting it as the largest church building program in modern history, the lead pastor of the church reportedly said, "The finest facility in this area should be one that glorifies almighty God,"[2] and that our "building program is not an end in itself, it is a means to an end to better minister to and meet the needs of the community."[3]

This pastor's heart may be filled with good intentions. But I can't help but ask the question: meet the needs of which community? The answer seems obvious. It will meet the needs of the community who is willing to come to church or who is already coming, a demographic that represents less than one-third of our nation. It's worthwhile to invest in our own people, but if we're called to love our neighbor as we love ourselves, I just can't help but wonder how much is *too* much. Whatever it is, I hope we can at least agree that we spend *way* more on ourselves than we do on reaching, serving, and loving those outside the church.

> It's not really about *how much* we spend; it's *what* we spend it on and what we can't do when the money is gone.

Many pastors believe that if we build it, they will come. Although studies show it's a radically shrinking demographic, we still believe that our "field of dreams" can be a means to an end. I'd be willing to bet that our non-Christian onlookers disagree. I believe they often look upon how we spend money in the church with some disdain. It's not really about *how much* we spend; it's *what* we spend it on and what we can't do when the money is gone.

Let's be honest. We'll hire a secretary or an office manager before we'll hire a pastor dedicated solely to mission and community outreach. We'll cut funding for a missionary, a church plant, or an adoption fund way before we'll cut the media or creative budget for Sunday morning. If we truly love our neighbor as ourselves, something we claim to be central to our existence, surely we can do something more significant with 130 million dollars.

Faith can be confusing enough without adding to the mix. Sorting through an unexpected death, processing a tragic natural disaster, or observing evil in the world are things that have shaken individuals' faith for centuries. People outside the church don't see hope in a building or a program. They don't value them like we do because they don't connect them with a nostalgic faith moment like we do. Culture has shifted. Things have changed. The church is on the fringe of our society, and we need to find new ways to undo the damage to our reputation. We have to change the way we are seen by the world. We have to become good news again.

MOTIVATION

One of the surprising realities of serving the least is that we can easily have more unbelievers join us in serving than would visit our church on a given Sunday morning. It's much less threatening to an unbelieving neighbor or friend to be invited to serve the homeless or help "make over" a classroom at an underresourced elementary school than to be invited to church. They most likely already believe in doing some good. But they don't yet see their need for the church.

With that in mind, our Restore Communities are often as diverse as those who attend our service projects. Many are found to be a refreshing mix between believers, seekers, and skeptics. We have people who grew up Catholic mixed with those whose parents were Jehovah's Witness. There are those who left church fifteen years ago and those who've never been. Some don't attend our church (or any church) on Sunday. Because of that foundation, those who come to faith or regain their faith often come with a stronger understanding of *being* good news than many people who have spent years in the church, listening to messages and sitting in the seats. When it's the gospel you receive, it's the gospel you intuitively live.

Serving the least can be really messy. It can be frustrating. And at times it can feel thankless. We know God is sharpening us through the experience. We know he's changing our hearts. We know we're obeying the commands of Jesus. But when the "newness" of selfless service wears off, it's hard to keep going. Many give up.

While obedience to the commands of Jesus should be enough to motivate us to serve others, it's often not. Our hearts must be awakened so that we crave more. Why? Because there *is* more. Deep inside the heart of every believer there is this draw toward something supernatural. We want to see lives radically changed because we know the gospel can radically change lives. If we do not find that place, that place of concern for the eternal salvation of souls, our service will always fall short. This is by design.

If we do not find that place, that place of concern for the eternal salvation of souls, our service will always fall short.

I remember finding that place of concern.

I had just read a blog critiquing social action, suggesting that it always fell short when it lacked an intentional act of spoken evangelism. The claim being made was that an act of mercy or kindness to someone in need has *no value* unless you attempt to somehow "close the deal" spiritually. The writer connected his thoughts on this matter with evidence from the historical movement often associated with theological liberalism—what is sometimes labeled *the social gospel*.

This writer's critiques were eerily similar to some of the same projects we had engaged in recently as a part of our Serve Austin Sunday efforts, so I quickly became defensive. But I also began to engage in the mental Olympics of panning through all the reasons we are committed to serving the least as a part of a holistic ministry approach.

There are at least three major beliefs that are tied in with the historical social gospel that clearly fall short of the teaching of Scripture. First, those who embraced the social gospel believed that somehow through their restorative efforts Christians could speed up the second coming of Jesus. They believed that their actions were hastening the final arrival of the kingdom of God. Second, they wrongly believed that social action, *apart from the gospel*, was the answer to the needs of people. They focused their efforts on addressing the problems of poverty, racial tensions, and the peril of war, but the focus on these problems replaced any personal responsibility for evangelism. Finally, they believed that building God's kingdom could be reduced to a matter of "technique and program." In the end, the kingdom could be established through human effort, apart from the supernatural work of God's Spirit.[4]

To be clear, not one of these views matches our beliefs as a church or our motivation for serving the least. I raise them to remind us that there are dangers in balancing the tension between the "good news" of serving the poor through social action and evangelistic proclamation. Historically, it has been a struggle for the church to find that balance, and this issue continues to be somewhat divisive when it comes up. In fact, it wasn't until I began processing this critique and examining my defensive attitude that I realized how much I had ignored the tension.

Austin New Church is a *socially active* church. Our prayer is that as we serve those in need, we might somehow represent the hands and feet of Christ to them. But we are also a *proclaiming* church. We hope that somehow, through our preaching and speaking, we might represent the voice of Christ as well. I have found the three assertions that Tim Chester and Steve Timmis make about the relationship between evangelism and social action in their book *Total Church* particularly helpful for clarifying our identity as a church body:

1. Evangelism and social action are distinct activities.
2. Proclamation is central.
3. Evangelism and social action are inseparable.[5]

While we must recognize the difference between evangelism and social action, we must make every effort to avoid separating them out, while retaining a priority on proclamation. In short, we need to develop a better understanding of the gospel and how it is both a message we announce and a reality we display to a lost and broken world. We both proclaim and become good news to the broken. As Tim Keller writes in *Generous Justice*, "A concern for justice in all aspects of life is neither an artificial add-on nor a contradiction to the message of the Bible."[6] We catch glimpses of the gospel in acts of mercy and justice. But when those acts are never connected to the hope of redemption and restoration through the work of Christ, we miss the point.

A healthy balance is found in the larger redemptive story. When we focus on just a small part of that story, we easily lose our balance. And along with it, we lose the power God has given us. This was the problem with the social gospel; social action became the singular purpose of the movement. Their entire gospel was focused on meeting needs and fixing physical problems, but it ignored the real spiritual needs of people. It was not the *whole* gospel. Yet, as we avoid the mistakes of the past, we must also learn to see that while social action is *not* the gospel, it is a necessary and biblical part of a complete gospel proclamation.

> We simply cannot separate our social responsibility and personal response from a doctrinally sound and holistic gospel.

Keller expresses the three "perspectives" of the gospel as being (1) doctrinal, (2) personal, and (3) social, while suggesting that any one or two of these perspectives emphasized by itself leads to a distortion of the gospel of Christ. In other words, right doctrine without appropriate application is incomplete. Giving our personal story without the reason for our hope and its impact is incomplete. And engaging in social action without the proper biblical motivation and perspective is also incomplete. We simply cannot separate our social responsibility and personal response from a doctrinally sound and holistic gospel. Keller writes, "The gospel, therefore, creates a people with a whole alternate way of being human ... These three 'perspectives' are all biblical and should be kept together. There is a tendency for Christians and churches to focus on just one of these perspectives and ignore the others. However, they are inseparable and inter-dependent on one another."[7]

But this raises the question: If evangelism and social action are so inseparable, *why is it so hard to see where they most naturally connect?*

I believe the answer to this question and the problem that has plagued the American church in the modern age lies in our understanding of what it means for us to be "good news" to people and how we share that message. As with anything, the messenger can easily get in the way of the message. I would suggest that this requires changing something about the messenger, but not the message. Let me give you an example.

Just yesterday I received a voice mail from a traveling evangelist. Although I had never heard of him, he was quick to let me know that he was a pretty big deal (roll eyes here). He started by offering a list of events he had spoken at, name-dropped a bit, then let me know he had sent an email about a month earlier that I didn't respond to. Not a good start.

He was going to be in the Austin area on an upcoming trip, and he wanted to let me know he'd be willing to come to our church for a Thursday night event. He was pretty direct about coming to "bless our fellowship" and that we could just "bless him" by helping offset some of the cost of his "tour" with a love offering.

Presumptuous? Check.

Arrogant? Check.

Borderline condescending? Check.

My return message clearly stated that I didn't think it would fit into what we were doing as a church and that I appreciated the offer and wished him well. Nevertheless he continued to call me back until I finally answered. After an hour on the phone, I returned to my work.

Now there is a possibility that that man's heart and his ministry are awesome. He may truly be called of God to do what he does and may be effective in certain environments. One thing I'm certain of is that he believed with all his heart that his coming to our church would be "good news" to us.

But at that very moment, he wasn't good news to me. Honestly, he was a bit annoying. He had no concern for whether or not I had the time to sit there and listen to him. And the truth was that I couldn't wait to get off the phone. I was at the point where I would do just about anything to get him to stop talking. I literally came close to giving in and saying yes. Then it hit me. Is this how unbelievers sometimes feel about us and what we have to offer them?

We truly think—in fact, we confidently *know*—that we have good news to share. We know in our hearts that it can change their lives. We believe that if we can just push a little more, people might cross that line of belief. And so we decide that even if we run the risk of ticking them off a bit, it's better to go ahead and do it. After all, we don't want to deny Jesus. We must live up to the slogan on our T-shirt: "I am not ashamed of the Gospel." We can't back down because it makes us uncomfortable: "His pain. Your gain." So we press the news, even when it seems an awkward fit for the context and the relationship.

We know we have good news. But that doesn't automatically mean we *are* good news.

Knowing the difference matters.

When someone doesn't share our priorities and doesn't really know us, forcing them to listen to us may not come across as good news. When we don't have the relational context or trust with someone who knows our heart and our motive, there are times when our words can do more damage than good.

SAYING AND DOING

We've already established that the gospel demands both proclamation and incarnation. Proclaiming has many forms, but in the end they are all *spoken*. Incarnation also has many forms, but it is always about *how* we live. It's good news when we speak the gospel message and share the offer of redemption that is available through Christ. And it's good news when we live incarnationally and take on the posture of Christ to others, humbly serving them. Either approach can be productive. But depending on *how* we engage in these activities, either of them can also be ineffective.

Proclamation and incarnation are inseparably linked together. A spoken word can quickly be discredited through our actions, and in the same way our actions can quickly validate the message we speak. We can try to argue that our actions and words function independent of one another, without consequence. But one thing is for certain: our observers never separate the two.

> A spoken word can quickly be discredited through our actions, and in the same way our actions can quickly validate the message we speak.

There are circumstances when proclamation is in order. We should always be prepared to speak and give a defense for the hope that we profess. There are moments when a spoken word can bring the conviction of sin and the confidence of reconciliation between a fallen child and a forgiving Father. But there are also times when speaking the good news must begin by living it out and showing people what it looks like.

Mercy and justice ministry is a life mate to the spoken word in this equation. In an increasingly post-Christian and postmodern context where moral authority trumps positional authority, we would be wise to make sure that our deed matches our creed. If our actions and our message do not align, the message we desperately want to be heard will not be heard—at least not in the way we want.

I wish I could say that I intuitively trust what I just wrote. But like many of you, I easily struggle with the insecurity of not doing or saying enough. After reading that overly critical blog, not only did I get defensive, I privately began to question our method.

Lame.

That very Sunday I was standing outside the front doors prior to our worship gathering. I was greeting people as they came in, but on this day I was also praying what became another game-changing prayer for me:

> *God, this was your idea. I trust what you're doing. But can you remind me that you're in this and that this is real? I need that right*

now. I know you don't have to, but will you show me how serving
the least can be connected directly with someone coming to Jesus?
Thanks. Amen.

As I look back now, it's a bit embarrassing. Up to this point we
had seen the fruit of conversion and transformation like nothing
I'd ever experienced. Yet I was feeling vulnerable and insecure as a
leader. I was worried about what others were thinking. And I needed
a shot of confidence.

I was literally asking God to throw me a bone.

At the conclusion of my prayer, I looked up and saw a young
couple with two children approaching the building. Honestly, they
looked homeless. The dad had a long unkempt beard with tattoos
down both arms. The mom seemed unsure and out of place. Both
kids were dressed in unmatched clothes that were anything but
clean.

I knew they were visitors, so I tried to position myself to say hi.
They were almost to the front doors before I could make eye contact
with the dad and squeak out a "hello" before they passed by. He
quietly said hi, and they disappeared into the building.

Seemed fairly insignificant at the time. But it wasn't.

Four months earlier, as a part of our vision to "Love Your Neighbor and Serve Your City," one of our Restore Communities, led by
Matthew Hansen (cofounder of Restore Austin), chose to partner
with an organization called Care Communities. Care Communities
is an amazing nonprofit based out of Austin that helps connect small
groups of people with families who have a family member dying
from cancer or AIDS.

Matthew's group was assigned to a young family with two children under the age of four. Both the mom and dad, Sarah and
Garrett, were HIV positive. Hard living doesn't come close to
describing their journey. A man and a woman who were once a
good-looking couple were now marked by a life-changing condition
and a meth addiction that had claimed nearly all of Sarah's teeth.
But her teeth were the least of their concern. Garrett was dying

from full-blown AIDS. They were as broken and helpless as anyone you'll ever meet.

The group's commitment was to divvy out their monthly calendar so that one or two couples from the Restore Community would be available to help the family each week. Sometimes it was to go grocery shopping, sometimes they helped with yard work or other household repairs, and often they just cleaned the house and helped with the laundry. This group did a great job of going above and beyond and even threw a birthday party for one of the kids.

Knowing how desperate the situation was, they selflessly served this family. Never did they lead on that the family had to do anything to "pay back" what they were receiving. They never made them feel like they had to come to church. They didn't require that they sit through an evangelism pitch in order to get their help. In fact, they didn't even tell them they were from a church. They just met their needs as they could, all along praying and hoping to be good news.

They didn't require that they sit through an evangelism pitch in order to get their help. In fact, they didn't even tell them they were from a church.

Three months into the partnership, Garrett approached Matthew...

Garrett: "Are you guys a church?"

Matthew: "Yeah, we are."

Garrett: "Well ... can we come to your church?"

Neither Sarah nor Garrett had any church background. Zero. Their children had never been inside the doors of a church building. And they were asking if they could come to ANC.

Since you've probably already put two and two together, I'll let the cat out of the bag. It was Sarah and Garrett who walked by me that morning right after my selfish prayer. It was their first visit to church, ever. I didn't know their story when they walked by. In fact, since all our Restore Communities serve on a regular basis — giving away as much time as they keep — I didn't even know the story of who this particular community was serving.

Two weeks later I knew their story. That week both Sarah and Garrett prayed to receive Christ. There are moments that the Spirit simply overwhelms me. This was one of them.

Four weeks after he received Christ, Garrett passed away. Sarah came to Matthew and told him she had no idea what to do next. She didn't have to. Their Restore Community surrounded her with love, took care of all the funeral arrangements, planned a service, and walked with her through the grieving. In that moment, the church became the church. The only people at the funeral were people from ANC. Had they not been there, Sarah would have been there alone … with her two young children.

One of my favorite passages of Scripture is also a passage that I sometimes don't know what to do with. It's stories like Sarah and Garrett's that help me understand and encourage me to action. It's found in 1 Peter 3, where Peter challenges us to be good news to people, to take the criticism of others, and to know that our faithfulness to God's calling and the way of Jesus is more important than being understood by our critics. And when we are good news, Peter says, people will find Christ. Sometimes, God will bless us in this way.

> Who is going to harm you if you are eager to do good? But even if you should suffer for what is right, you are blessed. "Do not fear their threats; do not be frightened." But in your hearts revere Christ as Lord. Always be prepared to give an answer to everyone who asks you to give the reason for the hope that you have. But do this with gentleness and respect, keeping a clear conscience, so that those who speak maliciously against your good behavior in Christ may be ashamed of their slander. For it is better, if it is God's will, to suffer for doing good than for doing evil. For Christ also suffered once for sins, the righteous for the unrighteous, to bring you to God.
>
> 1 PETER 3:13 – 18

I believe verse 14 gives us some helpful insight as to why evangelicals are often resistant to serving others and "doing good." Bottom line: we're afraid. We are afraid that it will cost us too much. We are afraid that it won't feel good or it will be too hard. We are afraid of being vulnerable and being labeled as those people who feed the hungry but never tell anyone about Jesus. We're afraid it just won't "work."

We need to see that much of this is really our "baggage," and it's cultural, not scriptural. Throughout the Gospels, Jesus calls us to do both: to serve the least and to be prepared to share the hope we profess. Peter knew this from having walked with Jesus and followed him firsthand. And he makes a strong connection between the two in this passage. He's reminding us that when we change what we do, even more than what we say, we'll also effectively change *how* people see us and view our actions.

Why is this true? Because serving those in need changes our posture to those we are serving, those we are serving with, and those who are watching from the outside. We become missionaries to our culture and not just evangelists. Yet the goal is similar: we become good news by engaging the need, whether it's physical, emotional, relational, or spiritual.

My good friends Hugh Halter and Matt Smay lead a faith community in Denver called Adullam, and they write about our posture as missionaries to our culture in *The Tangible Kingdom*:

> When your posture is wrong, you'll always be perceived to be an enemy or judge. When your posture is correct, you'll be perceived to be an advocate, a person who supports and speaks in favor of or pleads for another ... Instead of drawing a line in the sand and imploring them to "get right with God or get left behind," we step across from our religious side into their all-too-real world and ask how we can help.[8]

Peter is direct in telling us that if we do good, we will also need to be prepared to field questions. People will be curious. They will want what we have. In the words of Halter and Smay, "When you are as concerned about your posture as much as your message, people will move toward you."[9]

If you would have told me three years ago that people would actually ask me about my faith, ask me about my church, and ask me about Jesus ... all because I've taken an intentional posture of service, I would have told you that you're crazy. I probably would have warned you to be careful that you don't use "service" as an excuse to *not* share the gospel with someone. But I can tell you that it's true. This really happens. It does take a bit longer to build the trust that is needed, but the impact is far more powerful. People are hungry for the message we have to share. We don't have to convince them it's true — they've already seen it for themselves.

A few months ago I was working in my front yard when a neighbor walked by pushing her newborn baby in her stroller. She slowed down as she neared my house and said hello. I stood up and began to engage her in conversation, but I noticed that she was a bit distracted, as if she wanted to say something to me.

"So do you go to that church? That ANC church?"

It was obvious she didn't know that I was the pastor so I just replied, "Yes, I do."

"I hear you guys do some really good stuff."

"Really? That's great! I'm glad you've heard that," I replied.

"Um, can I go to your church?"

It was really hard to hold back showing a little emotion at the time. I was honored that she knew what we were about. I was humbled that she thought we represented something good. And I was encouraged that she had a desire to come.

MISSIONARIES TO OUR CULTURE

Hugh Halter and Matt Smay do an excellent job in their recent book, *AND: The Gathered and Scattered Church*, of describing what many consider to be a natural "missional flow" and what that might look like in missional-incarnational community. They show the pattern of how a missionary engages an unchurched society or unreached people group:

If you want your existing church to successfully engage the culture, you don't begin by telling your people to engage and then bring 'em to church. You must start by creating a new environment for them that provides a better witness to the culture and is the best way to see the kingdom lived out in concrete ways.[10]

I'm convinced that this understanding is foundational. It's what supports the vision of a Barefoot Church ... what it means to be a Barefoot Christian. We engage the culture by engaging the needs of that culture. We have to do this on their turf, not ours.

We engage the culture by engaging the needs of that culture.

One of the challenges of our existing church structures is that we are inclined to view service as an event or a program instead of viewing it as a way of life. Correcting this faulty understanding of service just might be one of the most difficult tasks in the church today. We tend to like events and programs. They are neat, tidy, and easily planned and controlled. We can budget for them and can measure their success. We can check all the boxes on our list, and when they are done, we can return to our "normal" lives.

But as much as we might want them to, events and programs don't transform lives. Willow Creek Community Church in Chicago spent plenty of time and resources figuring that out with their recent "Reveal" study. In the end, they learned that programs alone don't change lives and that numeric growth does *not* equal spiritual growth.[11]

There is a type of natural movement that we only engage when we let go of control. Maybe that's what Jesus meant when he reminded Peter that whatever he set loose on earth would be loosed in heaven (Matthew 16:19). In fact, our greatest challenge as a church has been moving that core biblical call to love our neighbor from the "scheduled event" realm to the "way of life" realm. We're trying to move it out from the thumb of an organized top-down plan and into the hands of smaller communities serving our city together.

We all know there's something more that has to happen beyond an invite to a Sunday morning gathering. Regardless of how great our gatherings might be, we need something even more effective and engaging. A recent study in our city of Austin showed that of all the methods pastors reported as being effective in reaching their community, "inviting to church" ranked a horrid ninth place out of a total of ten strategies listed. Ironically, in that same study, a majority of those same pastors reported that they still spent a majority of time and money for "outreach" on direct mail-outs and other methods to encourage their people to invite others to events and programs. If we really want to reach the people who tell us they will not come to us, this just doesn't add up.[12]

Instead, we must find ways of moving beyond the "event" of Sunday morning and the programmed weekdays. I can tell you that when we make that shift, our Sundays and our programs will be even better. But this won't happen by accident. Pastors and church leaders must make it a priority, create new structures, and give their people permission to live on mission. When they do, the service events we provide will encourage and support them as they begin to learn intuitively to recognize the deeper needs that need to be addressed and to meet those needs in a rhythm that is natural to the flow of daily life.

This is exactly what happened with Janet.

Last year during a prayer time for my Restore Community, Susan, a hospice nurse, asked us to pray for a new patient of hers named Mr. Nichols. Mr. Nichols was dying from cancer and was completely alone. She asked if any of us had some spare time to make the twenty-minute drive out to his house and just sit and listen to him talk, to please do so.

She let us know that he was about as grumpy a man as you'd ever meet and that whatever we did, not to tell him we were with a church and most certainly (to me) not to tell him that I was a pastor. Mr. Nichols had a reputation for kicking out hospice chaplains. He wanted absolutely nothing to do with religion.

So a handful of our people began visiting Mr. Nichols. Some of the guys did some repair work on his car. Some yard work was taken care of. Some of the gals brought food, helped clean up a bit around the house, and others just spent time with him. Janet, one of our newer Restore Community members, made an unlikely connection with Mr. Nichols, and somehow that grumpy old man found his way into her heart.

After a few weeks, Janet asked me if I thought it would be crazy to invite Mr. Nichols to move into her house with her family. He was bed-bound, and she had a plan to hire an ambulance, move his hospital bed into her dining room, and let him stay there until he passed away. She said she was freaking out and had never done anything like this before, but she just couldn't stand the thought of him dying alone.

It was hard to understand why the Spirit was leading in this way. To put it bluntly, Mr. Nichols wasn't just grumpy — he was downright mean! He was unappreciative. He was living alone because he had gone through a brutal divorce, and for unknown but connected reasons neither of his sons had spoken to him for over thirty years. Yet Janet continued to pray for him and serve him.

I'll never forget that Monday when Janet called and asked me to come down and sit with Mr. Nichols. She said that he was dying, and she wanted to take her children out of the house so they didn't have to see the medics come and take him away. Honestly, I was a bit scared to go at it alone. So I called Tray, my associate pastor, friend, and neighbor, to go with me. And we just sat there with him.

Mr. Nichols looked horrible. His breathing was incredibly irregular. Weighing less than eighty pounds, he just lay on the bed — silent, eyes closed, almost unconscious. His mouth was dry and cracked. My job was to take a sponge and wet his lips every few minutes to keep them from bleeding. I felt completely helpless. I think Tray did too. So we went to the other room and we prayed.

God, we don't know what to do. We're so thankful for this family to have taken Mr. Nichols into their home. We know you're doing something amazing in their life. But he's already outlived what anyone thought he would. I can't believe he's still alive. When he's conscious, he's in pain. When he's unconscious, everyone around him is in pain for him.

I don't know if he'll ever be conscious again. I don't know if it's even possible that he'll get a chance to respond to your grace. But, God, please forgive me if this is wrong to pray ... but if he's not going to come to know you, will you just let him die? If he is, will you give us a chance to share hope?

That's it, God. Amen.

That was a tearful prayer of desperation. We didn't know what to do next, so we just went back into the room with Mr. Nichols and sat next to his bed. Within fifteen seconds Mr. Nichols opened his eyes, sat up in bed, and looked straight at me as if we had been talking all day.

"You know," he said, "There's only one thing that matters when it's all said and done."

Gulp.

"What's that?" I replied.

"That you make your peace with the Man," he finished.

My heart pounded.

"Mr. Nichols," I cautiously added, "have you made your peace with the Man?"

He silently shook his head no. I looked at Tray. I honestly couldn't believe what was happening. It felt like a dream. So I looked back at Mr. Nichols and asked him if he'd like too. He nodded yes.

I spent the next few minutes sharing Christ with Mr. Nichols. I think the Spirit enabled me to be about as concise as I've ever been. He sat there quietly listening to all I said. Then when I asked him if this was a truth he'd like to receive, he nodded again, "Yes."

So we prayed. It was a simple prayer of confession. It was both a confession of sin and a confession of Christ as his Redeemer. While it seemed that Mr. Nichols was working hard to "mean all he was praying," at one moment I wondered if he had fallen asleep. But as

I brought the prayer to a close and said "Amen," he opened his eyes, glared straight into mine, and whispered quietly, "Amen."

Janet herself claims that she's never done anything like that before in her life. She's never made ministry so personal. But it was certainly the structure of serving together in community that even put the idea in her mind to engage ministry more personally.

I don't claim to fully understand how Janet's decision to rearrange her life played a role in Mr. Nichols' coming to faith. But I do know that our involvement did something to change how he felt about the church. Somehow we earned the right to be heard. Maybe God would have given him that same opportunity elsewhere; it's a bit arrogant to assume that we are the only conduit in which God can accomplish his work. But I'll tell you this, God showed up. It was tangible. And that experience changed all of us.

I have a good friend who says that "people don't care what you know until they know how much you care." You've probably heard that before. You've probably even agreed with it.

It's pretty cliché, but it nicely summarizes what we're talking about. While there will be moments when the Spirit leads us to share Christ directly and immediately—and we must be ready and willing to do so—we simply cannot ignore the fact that it takes intentional focus and dedication to be an effective missionary to our culture. In order to be good news, we need to rediscover what that means and must assume a different posture when we relate to the world around us. The majority of Americans have already counted out the church, and they instantly tune out when we jump into our Christian rhetoric. These are the people who openly tell us that they would never visit a church even if a good friend invited them. They are the increasingly vocal and skeptical majority of people in America.

SALT AND LIGHT

Jesus was clear that his followers were the salt of the earth, a light to the world, and a city on a hill that could not be hidden. Being a visible city or a shining light does not mean that we should talk even louder when no one is listening to us or that we should wave our arms and jump around when we aren't being seen, just to get in someone's face. When we are "salt," saltiness is part of our very nature. If we are indeed "light," we will indeed be seen in a dark world. Who we are can't be hidden because light consumes the darkness.

These are images that define the nature of a community that becomes good news to others. This is something we become because of what we believe, what we value, and what we do. Jesus tells us in Matthew 5 that when people encounter such a community, they will "see" our "good deeds" and then ultimately "glorify your Father in heaven" (Matthew 5:16).

The more the church lives in faithfulness to God and the gospel, the more visible God's grace will be for all those who long for it.

In a post-Christian society, this is what the church needs to become yet again: salt and light to the world. The unchurched community no longer expects much from church; in fact, they often expect the worst. They are jaded. Wounded. And confused. Yet people are still looking for hope, and no one else can offer what we have to offer them. Our story made public, the visible witness of our lives together as a whole community, is integral to whether or not our message of hope becomes their message of hope.[13]

To minister with influence in our current context, we must learn to locate the key differences between what our culture sees and what the kingdom of God made visible has to offer them. The more the church lives in faithfulness to God and the gospel, the more visible God's grace will be for all those who long for it. As Darrell Guder wrote in his book *Missional Church*,

Churches that listen to sermons deploring crime may be faithful in attending to God's call for right relationships among humanity. But the church that sets up victim-offender reconciliation programs and promotes equitable economic opportunities for communities where crime is the main escape route from financial despair is not only faithful but a remarkable light to the world, a city on a hill.[14]

Billy Graham, the most well-known evangelist of the twentieth century, understood that the cultural context was shifting. In an interview by author Gabe Lyons, Mr. Graham made this game-changing statement:

> Back when we did those big crusades in football stadiums and arenas, the Holy Spirit was really moving—and people were coming to Christ as we preached the Word of God. But today I sense something different is happening. I see evidence that the Holy Spirit is working in a new way. He's moving through people where they work and through one-on-one relationships to accomplish great things. They are demonstrating God's love to those with love, not just with words, but in deeds.[15]

Ed Stetzer recalls going through the personal challenge of understanding the relationship between evangelism and social justice while planting his first church among the urban poor in Buffalo, New York. In doing so, he had well-intentioned believers tell him to avoid being involved in social action because it would detract from the gospel. They warned him specifically about the dangers of liberation theology (by name) and told him to be sure to preach Jesus.

"I found," said Stetzer, "that I could not preach Jesus and not care about justice. And, if I wanted real justice, I had to preach Jesus. They did not seem separable, but history has shown that they can be."[16]

I have a close friend who started an organization to help improve the condition of orphanages in India. It's a holistic effort that covers everything from education, to clothing and food, to faith. But they don't lead with verbal evangelism; they lead with addressing physical need to address head-on their impoverished state.

When I first met her, I asked why they do that. She simply said this, "Anyone you meet in India who is hungry will accept your Jesus if you have food. Honestly, it's become a bit of a joke among the poor in the areas we serve." It's like they've been inoculated by

Serving the least doesn't get in the way of evangelism that isn't already happening. It only opens more doors.

our Christian rhetoric. Similar to learning a new dialect of an old language, they have found they must discover new ways to share their faith. They lead through engaging the greatest need in their country, and people are still coming to Christ.

Some believe that serving the least will never lead to conversion. This is untrue. Compassion without motive has proven time and again to create a bridge to sharing faith. Serving the least doesn't get in the way of evangelism that isn't already happening. It only opens more doors. There is a connection. It can lead to earning the right to be heard. But it doesn't end there; it can also play a major role in restoring a broken faith.

THE DECHURCHED AND JADED

There are plenty of people with a broken faith. They too have become skeptics in their own right — not necessarily skeptics of faith, but more often, skeptics of church. It's often a once-committed believer who has left the organized church. These are the dechurched of America. They're typically the ones who have given all they had to a church somewhere only to have been disappointed or disillusioned by what they experienced.

It's estimated that the number of unchurched Americans is growing by about one million each year. According to the American Religious Identification Survey, the percentage of Americans with no religious preference doubled over the last decade. "However, less than 40 percent were atheists; the other 60 percent claimed to be 'religious' or 'spiritual.'" What does this tell us? "Plenty of people in this country are interested in spiritual matters. They are simply not going to church to feed this interest."[17]

We've reacquainted with a number of Christians and once-upon-a-time church attenders through serving regularly with nonprofits. Many have left not just so they can do more, but because of the criticism they've endured for allowing it to take the place of regular programs and ministries that build up the existing structures of the church.

Julia Duin, religion reporter and author of *Quitting Church: Why the Faithful Are Fleeing and What to Do about It,* wrote about this trend: "None . . . wanted to quit church; they felt pushed out or that leaving was taking the high road. 'Many of us dropouts tried to work behind the scenes to keep unity, but if we spoke out, we were in rebellion. Many of us chose to leave rather than start wars.' "[18]

As pastors and church leaders, we need to wake up. This is a sad and sobering reality. There are many of these walking wounded in our communities looking for a reason to believe in the church again. And our traditional forms of church are not reaching them. In fact, reaching the dechurched will likely require taking the same posture that we take to reach the unchurched. It's not because they haven't heard the gospel; it's because they don't trust what they see. They have lost faith in the church, and they are suspicious of American Christianity. But this is not just their problem. This is our problem as well.

I know many people who just wanted to serve their neighborhoods and communities in ways they felt equipped, called, or within their passions. Yet when they shared this desire with church leaders, they felt isolated and went outside the church to find people willing to serve with them. While we may rightly be concerned about people who readily abandon the church community, I believe we must also take a good look at ourselves. Have we fallen so far into serving ourselves, our structures, and our agenda that we no longer have room for those who want to pour themselves completely out in creative and fresh ways?

Here's the dilemma we face: the more people grow in their faith, the less they will depend on our structures. The more we challenge them to serve, the less they will value our programs. This is exactly what the Bible says will happen. If a mark of a disciple is one who is on mission, then by our very nature, we must be sent. If it's not our goal to send them, they will eventually leave anyway.

Recently we had a family visit ANC after spending a few years recovering from a prior church experience. They were jaded. They had lost hope in the church. The mother wrote this:

> I have not met you personally yet, but have been visiting for a few months. We had been looking to start back to church when a friend mentioned ANC.
>
> I mentioned the phrase "start back" to church, because I fall into the "discouraged by my last church experience" group. We were members there for ten years, but the last year or two we were there, I had become disappointed in organized religion and began questioning everything. It just worked out nicely that we moved to Austin when I was at my most uncomfortable and I just took a two-year break.
>
> Our experience with ANC has been faith-changing for me and has come at a time when I wasn't sure organized religion had any redeeming or genuine qualities. I hadn't really given up faith in God, but I had almost completely given up faith in human ability to actually do something sincere, productive, and unselfish when in an organized religious setting.
>
> I love that you all get it. That you acknowledge human weakness and try to work around those faults by simply moving on to what is important. I love that you realize what needs to be done as far as using time and resources to affect your community and actually make a difference in the world ... that it is actually about human kindness, concern, and sharing in every sense of the word. I love the holistic approach you are taking by attacking injustice, sharing God's teaching and coming together as a group (a Christian community) to do all of it.
>
> You and your church community have begun to restore my faith that a church can be a haven and a place where you can trust others and take them at face value and work together to learn about God, worship, and try to make a difference in your community and the world.

What an amazing journey. I was thankful for her candor about her prior church experience—and even more thankful for being concise about what drew her back. She was looking for something of significance, a place that shared her values and priorities. To her, that was summed up by being a place of worship *and* mission. She wasn't running from being a committed believer. She wasn't looking for a place to coast and be comfortable; she was looking for a place to make a difference. A place that empowered her and encouraged her to live a life sent.

Trace and Shonna grew up in church. They were leaders in their youth group and were high school sweethearts. As young adults, they went through a personal and painful church experience that led them to leaving. After trying to find their "fit" elsewhere for a season, they finally decided church just wasn't for them. They believed in God but had lost faith in the church. And they were struggling with whether or not God was the God most Christians believed he was.

Trace and Shonna spent more than twelve years away from faith community. They found their way to ANC a little over a year ago. They have a beautiful family of five and are now in the process of adopting through the foster care system. Their story offers an amazing picture of a restored faith. They now lead a Restore Community and volunteer regularly as active partners in everything we do. And they have become some of our best friends.

Not long ago Trace and I were having a conversation on the significance of serving the poor and people returning to the church. Following our conversation, he sent me an encouraging email elaborating on what he shared:

> Brandon,
>
> I've been thinking about our talk the other night and just wanted to make sure you knew how much I value being a part of a church that actually does what it says it's about. My big problem with church ... the thing that made me think I was never going back ... was that I perceived the church to be a

bunch of people who were saying they believed one thing, but then they did another. They said they believed in Jesus, but then they didn't act like him. They showed up dressed in their finest on Sunday mornings and paraded around trying to impress one another. Meanwhile, I'm reading the Bible and it's got a different message.

Of course, some of that was just about things like hypocrisy and judgment. But some of it was about the fact that Jesus is saying "Love your neighbor as yourself," and no one in the church is doing that.

So when I heard that ANC actually cancelled services to "be the church" by serving around the city, I was blown away. (What, no parading around in our best trying to impress each other??) To me, that proved that ANC stood behind its convictions. Add that ingredient to being "real" and admitting that we're all sinners, and I knew I had to really give it a chance.

Now, as important as the social action was to me, it was even more important to Shonna. She had been trying to talk me into serving more with our family before we ever heard of ANC. She just had a heart for community service (not in the running for City Council way ... but in the helping poor people way). She had really been on me to do that for about a year. Looking back, I feel that was God's plan, leading us through her heart for service to ANC. Because it was her heart for service that immediately hooked her, and then she dragged me along to see for myself.

Good stuff man. Trace

The acceptance of "doing good" is not only an expectation of our culture but an opportunity. People applaud generosity, yet they don't expect the church to be generous. Reggie McNeil wrote in *Missional Renaissance*:

> The explosion of good actually creates a chance for the church
> to gain relevance and influence. But only if the church is willing

to get out of the church business and get over the delusion that the "success" of the church impresses the world. It does not. It only impresses church people, while making others even more skeptical of the church's true motives.[19]

We live in a world that is watching the church with one eyebrow raised. When Hollywood is viewed as doing more to feed the hungry and fight human trafficking than the church, we need to take a hard look at what we're doing and ask if it's enough. Jesus taught that when others see our good deeds they would assign value to God (Matthew 5:16). I can't help but think that the same is true for his church.

CHAPTER 6

Expanding our Understanding of Discipleship

My kids do pretty well in school. They get that from their mom. Each of them has issues with talking too much and being the class clown. They get that from me. Thankfully, their ability to do well in school has overcome their temptation to crack jokes and be a distraction. And they typically get straight As on their report cards.

Last year, Gavin, my seventh grader, brought home a progress report with everything above a 94 percent except one 62 percent in biology. I was ticked. Before I had the chance to string him up in the back yard, Jen began to talk with him about what was going on.

After a few minutes of lecture and at the first sign of her taking a breath, he blurted out, "Come on, Mom, it's my first D!"

With great wisdom, she replied, "Let me ask you a question, do you think a murderer could stand in court before a judge and say, 'C'mon judge, that was my first murder'?"

Silence.

"Mom, are you comparing my D to murder?"

He had a point there. They both burst out laughing.

Turns out Gavin hadn't murdered anyone. That was a relief. But he did forget to turn in one assignment, and two more had been "misplaced." After they were "found" and turned in, the grade was pulled up to an A. All was good.

Grades are funny. We place so much emphasis on a percentage that honestly, we rarely know the details that go into them. We just want them up. Just a handful of neglecting zeros, and a student who scored 100 on every other project could end up repeating a grade. One more zero and Gavin would have been failing.

Some of our discipleship efforts in the church deserve an A. In fact, it's impressive to see some of the spiritual development tracts, equipping courses, accountability groups, and Bible studies that are available to us. We have a conference, a retreat, a message series, and a small-group curriculum for anything the world can throw at us. But there are some glaring missing assignments, enough to pull down our grade significantly. And according to the statistics and percentages, we're not getting a passing grade. There are some huge gaps in our discipleship process.

In 1999, an international group of Christian leaders met in England with the hopes of coming away with a definition of discipleship. The Eastbourne Consultation Joint Statement on Discipleship was created and began with an acknowledgment of need: "As we face the new millennium, we acknowledge that the state of the Church is marked by growth without depth. Our zeal to go wider has not been matched by a commitment to go deeper."[1] John Stott has added his voice on this matter: "For many years, 25 or more, the church-growth school has been dominant. I rejoice in the statistics, but we must say it is growth without depth. I believe it was Chuck Colson who said the church is 3,000 miles wide and an inch deep. Many are babes in Christ."[2]

"The fruit of the Spirit is love, joy, peace, forbearance, kindness, goodness, faithfulness, gentleness and self-control" (Galatians 5:22–23). Yet bitterness, an unforgiving spirit, anxiety, and apathy abound. Studies show there is little, if any, difference between Christians and non-Christians regarding addiction, divorce, depression, volunteerism, or giving. This is something that should bother us. "This superficiality comes into startling focus when we observe the incongruity between the numbers of people who profess faith in Jesus Christ and the lack of impact on the moral and spiritual climate of our times."[3]

I grew up hearing that "20 percent of the church does 80 percent of the work." And that's just the way it is. I'm sad to report that the message has changed. I now hear more frequently that "10 percent of the church does 90 percent of the work." In a day where a disciple is often defined as the opposite of a consumer, we're consuming more and more. The more we consume, the less change we will see.

Studies show there is little, if any, difference between Christians and non-Christians regarding addiction, divorce, depression, volunteerism, or giving.

Pastors are not immune. Of the men leading the way, 70 percent constantly fight depression. Eighty percent of their adult children surveyed have had to seek professional help for depression, and 50 percent of pastors' marriages end in divorce.[4] We're failing to see transformation and the fruit of the Spirit, even in our leaders.

Where we send the most confusing message as Christians is in our lack of love for our neighbor and our love for one another. Jesus said that we would be known by our love for one another, yet we're most commonly known for our infighting. I'm too embarrassed to talk about some of the things I've heard said behind closed doors—the humiliation and floggings that can take place among some Christians.

No greater example is found than a simple scroll through the Facebook news feed during the recent presidential election. I almost deleted my account. It's way too easy to get sucked into all the trash that some Christ followers write. Some of it was plain hatred and ugliness. Hello, everyone; the entire world is watching. Use some discretion. Dab it with a little love while you're at it. It should sadden us to realize how far away we are from being like Christ. We truly are an imperfect people hanging desperately to a perfect Christ. We need to stop clinging to the "idea" of being transformed, and honestly, mournfully, and humbly ask him to break our hearts for the things that breaks his. The effort of our pursuit has to match the gravity of the idea. That's the place where we can be used and transformation begins.

> We need to stop clinging to the "idea" of being transformed, and honestly, mournfully, and humbly ask him to break our hearts for the things that breaks his.

HOLISTIC DISCIPLESHIP

When Jesus told us to go and make disciples, he meant that we would begin a new way of life. Yet most of us do not feel made new. Many of us feel like we're on the hamster wheel of spiritual formation, and nothing is changing. We're learning a lot, but we're not experiencing an equal amount of transformation. Greg Ogden offers seven marks of discipleship that can be used to identify the gap between the biblical standard and the reality of faith:

1. From passive participates to proactive ministers
2. From spiritually undisciplined to spiritually disciplined
3. From private faith to holistic discipleship
4. From blending in to a countercultural force
5. From church is optional to church is essential
6. From biblically illiterate to biblically informed
7. From shrinking from personal witness to sharing our faith[5]

At first glance, this seems like a list we would deem more appropriate for pastors and church leaders than for the common believer. For the rest of us, we've lowered the bar far too much, failing to embrace even one or two of these marks, much less all seven. If these are even a semblance of what truly marks a disciple, it's time to ask if what we're doing is really working.

Only as we soberly assess the way things are, can we have any hope of getting to the way things were designed to be. We have hope because Jesus as the Lord of the church seeks for his bride to be without spot and blemish, for through his church his life will be manifest. Christianity would be incredibly influential in our culture if Christians consistently lived their faith. Most non-Christians don't read the Bible, so they judge Christianity by the lives of the Christians they see. The problem is that millions of Christians don't live like Christians.[6]

For years church leaders have tried to come to a clear and agreeable understanding of discipleship. Along the way we've continued to run into snags only magnified by denominational or methodological preference. In order to advance the conversation, it might serve us best to identify some key needs facing our traditional forms of discipleship.

1. We Need to Believe We Can Change

We are simply not seeing the fruit of transformation at the rate we might claim, expect, and even hope for. It's more common to see our discipleship processes create the spiritually arrogant than a transformed people living on mission. We still feel the urge to "go deeper" and "be fed" although we may be in Bible studies three to four times a week. It's as if we're spinning our tires with the throttle to the floor, but we're not going anywhere. Yet, "his divine power has given us everything we need for a godly life through our knowledge of him who called us by his own glory and goodness" (2 Peter 1:3).

There was as similar situation revealed in the church at Corinth. Paul wrote to them:

> Brothers and sisters, I could not address you as people who live by the Spirit but as people who are still worldly—mere infants in Christ. I gave you milk, not solid food, for you were not yet ready for it. Indeed, you are still not ready. You are still worldly. For since there is jealousy and quarreling among you, are you not worldly? Are you not acting like mere humans?
>
> 1 CORINTHIANS 3:1–3

Paul reveals to them that whatever they were doing to grow their faith, it was not working. The evidence was not that they didn't know the law or their religious duty; it was the remainder of jealousy and quarreling in their community. Both are juvenile and selfish and are evidences of the flesh, not of the Spirit. The very fact that there was division in the church showed Paul that they were not ready to tackle the significant issues of mission.

The author of Hebrews gives us some insight as to why this might be happening:

> We have much to say about this, but it is hard to make it clear to you because you no longer try to understand. In fact, though by this time you ought to be teachers, you need someone to teach you the elementary truths of God's word all over again. You need milk, not solid food! Anyone who lives on milk, being still an infant, is not acquainted with the teaching about righteousness. But solid food is for the mature, who by constant use have trained themselves to distinguish good from evil.
>
> HEBREWS 5:11–14

As a parent there's nothing more liberating than when you break through a growth stage with an infant. There are several milestones that seem to accompany a sense of freedom for the parent, the child, or both. An infant begins to sleep through the night, or a toddler is finally potty trained. It was pretty liberating when our youngest headed off to kindergarten and when our oldest was old enough to babysit. But none was as meaningful as when a baby moves from milk and being hand-fed to solid food. There are a handful of significant things that happen in this moment: they can now learn to feed themselves, Mom and Dad are set free and the child is able to try a variety of other foods, and the opportunity to increase consumption triggers even more growth.

Hebrews reminds us that growing up is good. But there are some deficiencies we have that might stunt our growth.

We lack a sense of urgency. As parents we can't wait until our kids feed themselves. Church leaders are often so concerned and distracted by the things that keep the engine churning that we often place little value on the urgency of making disciples. Sunday comes every week, and we easily allow it to take precedence. And it's not just the fault of church leaders; as believers we are so consumed by everything else "church" that we neglect the time it takes to meditate on God's Word. Many of us only pick up the Bible once a week (if that) on Sunday mornings. "We have much to say about this, but it is hard to make it clear to you because you no longer try to understand" (Hebrews 5:11).

We lack the ability to feed ourselves. The goal of every disciple should be to learn how to feast on the Word of God without being completely dependent on an outside teacher. We should become so familiar with it that we become teachers ourselves. Most of our current discipleship rhythms create dependency, not trust and release. "In fact, though by this time you ought to be teachers, you need someone to teach you the elementary truths of God's word all over again" (Hebrews 5:12).

We feast too infrequently. When we are completely dependent on others, we're only getting a portion of what they have to offer. And we only get what they offer, when they offer it, nothing more. We consume what they have. We need Sunday morning, Sunday night, and Wednesday church or we starve. If we were to take the time to sit down and feast on Scripture ourselves, in addition to being under the teaching of other godly leaders, there is no limit to what we could digest. The fruit of this repetition is the fruit of the Spirit and an ability to discern right from wrong.

Believer, you have access to a Bible. Prayerfully read it, and keep reading it. Ask the Spirit to lead you and do whatever it says. It will change your life. "But solid food is for the mature, who by constant use have trained themselves to distinguish good from evil" (Hebrews 5:14).

2. We Need a More Holistic Understanding of Discipleship

There is a deficit in our collective understanding of what a disciple looks like. Maybe this is part of the problem. Some theologians understand it, and pastors have a vision for it, but most believers do not. We either oversimplify it to a reduced list of disciplines or overcomplicate it with terms only a seminary professor could understand. The Eastbourne Consultation Joint Statement on Discipleship attempted to capture it this way:

> While there are valid differences of perspective on what constitutes discipleship, we define Christian discipleship as a process that takes place within accountable relationships over a period of time for the purpose of bringing believers to spiritual maturity in Christ. Biblical examples suggest that discipleship is both relational and intentional, both a position and a process. We become disciples by turning from sin through repentance and turning to God through faith...
>
> The process of discipleship is played out in a vital life-giving relationship to God that enables us to walk in the light as He is in the light, and do the will of the Father (1 John 1:7; John 4:34). Jesus said if we hold to His teaching, then we are really His disciples (John 8:31), and we demonstrate this through loving one another (John 13:34–35).[7]

The statement goes on to identify the marks of a disciple:

> Although the process of identifying effective discipleship tools or methods is affected by the culture and setting, we affirm that
>
> 1. The life of a disciple is marked by submission to Christ. Jesus said that we cannot be His disciples unless we give up our very lives (Luke 14:27).
> 2. The marks of true repentance in the life of a disciple are evidenced by ongoing transformation, personal holiness, compassionate service, and the fruit of the Spirit (Galatians 5:22).
>
> We acknowledge that perfection will not be achieved until we see Him face to face. True disciples do fail and are marked by humble repentance in response to personal failure, but recognize God's forgiveness and restoration in the journey.[8]

That's a pretty involved statement. And it's worth noting that the document was revised six times prior to its release. "The mere fact that it was revised six times speaks to the lack of continuity in Christendom today regarding a most important facet of our faith, namely discipleship ... Their document, in its revisions and lack of specifics, only serves to illustrate there is a problem; and that being, a universal lack of real consensus and direction regarding discipleship."[9]

We should consistently consider new ways and new forms to draw closer to the image of Christ.

We may never find or develop a complete and concise enough list to please everyone and fit every context. This may be by design and part of our tension. We do, however, need to be aware that it presents a unique problem and should keep us in search of any and all missing elements. Maybe the search itself is part of the process. Discipleship is indeed "relational and intentional, both a position and a process." It must be communicated as a holistic effort that is all-engrossing. We should consistently consider new ways and new forms to draw closer to the image of Christ. This brings up a third need of discipleship.

3. We Need to Consider More Deeply What We're Neglecting

A few months ago I attended a leadership meeting walking us through how to develop strategic initiatives for ministry. The goal presented was to ultimately start with the end in mind. In other words, identify desired outcomes first, then work backward to develop a reasonable strategy to get there, one step at a time. The beauty of this process is found in its intuitively evaluative nature. You can't help but realize the goals are unrealistic or unattainable if you work your way back to the present and you're not at the same starting point as reality.

If we are to devise a successful strategy of disciple-making in our churches, we must first assess the gap between where we are and where we are called to go. Jesus promoted this approach when he challenged those who would follow him to first count the cost.

"Suppose one of you wants to build a tower. Won't you first sit down and estimate the cost to see whether you have enough money to complete it?" (Luke 14:28).

The Eastbourne Statement on Discipleship claims: "The marks of true repentance in the life of a disciple are evidenced by ongoing transformation, personal holiness, compassionate service, and the fruit of the Spirit."[10]

Essentially what they're offering is a list of four desired outcomes. Instead of starting where we are and evaluating discipleship by what we're doing, we should take a look at whether or not we're accomplishing what we hope to accomplish. What we'll find is that almost every biblical result of discipleship is something that is out of our hands. "We cannot change ourselves, just as we cannot change the world by ourselves. It is the Spirit's ministry to bring about changed lives, transformed communities, and redemptive ministry in the world. This reflects the duality of the church as an organization that is both holy and human."[11]

> We can gain all the knowledge in the world, but without the Spirit there will be no fruit, no transformation, no personal holiness, no compassionate service.

We need the Spirit more than we can fathom. We can gain all the knowledge in the world, but without the Spirit there will be no fruit, no transformation, no personal holiness, no compassionate service. Here's a not-so-secret secret: if you're a believer in the Son of God, the Holy Spirit lives inside of you. I'm convinced he's speaking as well. The question is this: Are we listening? I think we listen more than we'll admit. Honestly, it's rare that we come to a decision never having a sense for what is right. The Holy Spirit does not sit stagnant; he moves with conviction. In Thessalonians, Paul had to remind the church of this power:

> Because our gospel came to you not simply with words but also with power, with the Holy Spirit and deep conviction. You know how we lived among you for your sake. You became imitators of

us and of the Lord, for you welcomed the message in the midst
of severe suffering with the joy given by the Holy Spirit.

1 THESSALONIANS 1:5–6

We are experts at creating confusion and clouding clarity when
we want to justify our actions. I've purchased things, done things,
neglected things, said things, and thought things that I know were
not the best things to do—all along reasoning with myself, intentionally ignoring, and choosing not to listen. We choose not to pray about
such decisions because we already know the answer. We fool even
ourselves. But that's an easy thing to do when we want to be fooled.

Let's be honest for a moment. Knowing what we know about
God, does he really want us to serve the poor? Is there any chance
our lack of doing so negatively impacts our transformation? I would
argue yes. Is there any chance doing so would radically help it? I
would once again argue a resounding yes.

Take a moment to consider the pages of Scripture; take a year if
you need. Does he desire that we be agents of peace (Matthew 5:9),
ministers of reconciliation (2 Corinthians 5:18–19) and renewal
(Colossian 3:10)? Should we fight for the orphan (James 1:27) and
plead the case of the widow (Isaiah 1:17)? Does he really want us to
fight injustice (Isaiah 58:6)? Should we show mercy (Matthew 5:7)?

Ask God to search your heart, and ask the Spirit to speak.

Do me a favor. If your answer is no, then stop reading and throw
this book away. You're wasting your time. If your answer is yes, it
begs an additional question: Why don't we then? The only logical
answer is humbling: we simply choose our way over God's way.

Earlier we discussed how just one zero in a class can drop even a
perfect grade to a failing grade. The problem with our current forms
of discipleship is not necessarily found in what we do well; it's found
in what we've neglected. In many of our cases, it's the lack of chasing
the Spirit and the compassionate service that follows. Without them,
we will ultimately fail at both transformation and personal holiness.

We need to keep studying and memorizing Scripture. We need
to keep praying and holding each other accountable. We need to

continue spending seasons in topical and equipping Bible studies. And in addition to those things, we need to figure out how to delight in the ways of Jesus more often. We need to commit more of our ways to him (I suggest all of them). It's literally impossible to do so and choose the way of self.

> Take delight in the LORD,
>   and he will give you the desires of your heart.
> Commit your way to the LORD;
>   trust in him and he will do this:
> He will make your righteous reward shine like the dawn,
>   your vindication like the noonday sun.
>
> PSALM 37:4–6

4. We Need a Reproducible Process That's Willing to Let Go

At the very heart of discipleship is the spirit of recurrent disciple making. As long as our discipleship process remains rigid and dependent on its initiator, it will always fall short of its potential.

> Jesus saved every church considerable time and effort when he wrote the mission statement that gives us our marching orders: "Go therefore and make disciples of all nations" (Matthew 28:19). What is a disciple of Jesus but one who is self-initiating, reproducing and fully devoted to him? What seems unattainable is that there would be churches filled with disciples who do not have to be pushed, motivated and cajoled.[12]

This brings us back to our first point. Is it possible that we're not seeing the spiritual fruit of transformation resulting in self-motivation and devotion because we're not making true disciples? Are we creating codependent disciples? Codependency does not blossom; it does not reproduce; it only creates more codependency.

"We're a nation of consumers. And there's nothing wrong with that."

That's what the commercial said anyway. I'm not so sure that the credit card company who made it is a credible authority on telling us whether or not that's a problem. But at least they got the first part right — we're certainly consumers. The greatest enemy to reproducing disciples is our desire to consume. More times than not, we don't want to be released for ministry. We'd rather someone else provide what we need and just consume it. And it'd be nice to have some hot coffee waiting there too. It's a love-hate relationship, and it's killing any chance of our helping someone else experience what we've experienced. It's killing our hope of becoming disciples who make disciples.

THE WAY OF THE RABBI

Jesus was once asked point blank what we need to do to inherit eternal life; he was asked by someone who already knew all the rules. His response? Give to the poor. We know the law, yet this is probably the most obvious discipleship tool we miss.

> "You know the commandments: 'You shall not commit adultery, you shall not murder, you shall not steal, you shall not give false testimony, honor your father and mother.'"
>
> "All these I have kept since I was a boy," he said.
>
> When Jesus heard this, he said to him, "You still lack one thing. Sell everything you have and give to the poor, and you will have treasure in heaven. Then come, follow me."
>
> LUKE 18:20–22

I assure you, this wasn't about the cash. Jesus didn't need this man's money to help the poor. This man needed to help the poor himself. There is so much wrapped in what happens when we do. We are confronted at the very soul of our existence. This wasn't the first time Jesus encouraged this discipline for making disciples, and it wasn't his last time either.

> But when you give a banquet, invite the poor, the crippled, the lame, the blind, and you will be blessed. Although they cannot repay you, you will be repaid at the resurrection of the righteous.
>
> LUKE 14:13–14

In a moment, Zacchaeus discerned what Jesus required of him:

> But Zacchaeus stood up and said to the Lord, "Look, Lord! Here and now I give half of my possessions to the poor, and if I have cheated anybody out of anything, I will pay back four times the amount."
>
> Jesus said to him, "Today salvation has come to this house, because this man, too, is a son of Abraham."
>
> LUKE 19:8 – 9

Paul labeled Tabitha a disciple. Here are the marks of her discipleship: "In Joppa there was a disciple named Tabitha ... she was always doing good and helping the poor" (Acts 9:36).

The angel who came to Cornelius, the first Gentile convert reported in Scripture, claimed that the very reason he was there was because God not only heard his prayers, but remembered his service to the poor: "Cornelius answered: 'Three days ago I was in my house praying at this hour, at three in the afternoon. Suddenly a man in shining clothes stood before me and said, "Cornelius, God has heard your prayer and remembered your gifts to the poor"'" (Acts 10:30 – 31).

The apostles, pioneers of the New Testament church, knew that if they did anything of value, they should continue to serve the poor: "James, Cephas and John, those esteemed as pillars, gave me and Barnabas the right hand of fellowship when they recognized the grace given to me. They agreed that we should go to the Gentiles, and they to the circumcised. All they asked was that we should continue to remember the poor, the very thing I had been eager to do all along" (Galatians 2:9 – 10).

Believing is not just a matter of knowing. "Believing is also a matter of doing. Believing is trusting that Jesus' way of living is the right way, and trusting it enough that one is willing to live that way—and die that way."[13]

We've been talking about the elements of discipleship ad nauseum. Bible study, surrender, the Holy Spirit, giving back—no one would disagree with these marks of a disciple—but most people never transfer these practices from the church campus to an actual life. According to our role model, Jesus, surrender meant death in every possible way: materially, relationally, and physically. Surrender until there was nothing left but redemption for a broken world.

> The Holy Spirit is a blazing fire, charring every remnant of selfishness and pride left in our souls, an unquenchable fire that cannot be ignored or denied.

The Holy Spirit is a blazing fire, charring every remnant of selfishness and pride left in our souls, an unquenchable fire that cannot be ignored or denied. Giving back means giving all; any inferior definition is pure deception. Our money, our resources, our gifts, our time, our dreams, our selfish ambitions, our comfort—these we give back in their entirety. Anything less is not discipleship at all. It is simply a clever substitution by a crafty enemy who has figured out how to use our own weaknesses against us, rocking us to complacent sleep with a consumer version of the gospel and knowing all the while he is making goats out of sheep.

TANGIBLE TRANSFORMATION

Earlier today I sat down to start this chapter on how social action impacts discipleship when I was interrupted by a call from my wife. She said seven words, "Brandon. Come home. We got our referral!" Then she hung up.

Nearly a year ago we started the long journey of international adoption. After spending some time in Africa with The Eden Reforestation Projects and falling in love with the children of Ethiopia, our hearts were affirmed that that's where we were to adopt.

Jen handled the whirlwind of paperwork like a pro. It's like applying for twenty mortgages at the same time. Quite a process: family history, addresses, references, financial reports, physicals (even the dog), fingerprints, and home studies. We submitted our dossier and made the payments, thanks to some incredible friends and support-ers. And we waited. I tried my best not to think about it too often, hoping the time would pass. Jen's strategy was a little different; adop-tion blogs, Facebook groups, email chains, and the adoption agency website were a daily obsession for her.

Today we were given the names, faces, and heartbreaking stories of a beautiful little five-year-old girl and seven-year-old boy we were going to adopt.

There are experiences in life that simply change us. Some are good. Some are tragic. But they change who we are and what we're about from that point forward. While we've yet to realize the full impact adoption will have on us, this is certainly one of those experiences for us. Life will never be the same.

We seem to think discipleship is an agreement to knowledge instead of a commitment to a gospel that makes all things new.

Following Christ should change our lives. We should not be the same. Discipleship should be transforming. Yet when we think about our spiri-tual development, it's easier to see a change in our practices than in our passions. We continue to add things and replace things, yet our hearts remain the same. We seem to think discipleship is an agreement to knowledge instead of a commitment to a gospel that makes all things new.

I share my story because I want you to know that my hope is completely different today from where it was a handful of years ago. I've seen the same in others. While I know I have a ways to go, I can honestly say that the way I think is different. The way I feel is different. The way I love is simply different. My faith journey is now a joy. My church experience is life giving. And for the first time, I actually do life with the people I'm in biblical community with.

Most of us change over the years. Yet few can look back and identify supernatural God-level transformation and link it to a clear and concise discipleship process. When we add serving the least into the mix of our passion for God's Word, worship, and community, we take something already great and make it better.

I received an email the other day from one of the founding members of our church. His story is simple: an extremely successful businessman who's done just about everything in life and has been radically changed by serving the least. He writes:

> Brandon,
>
> Just wanted to put words to what's been going on in my life over the last few years and share it with you. You know that each time we do the homeless grill-out downtown, my post is at the front of the line handing out the tickets. I love it because I get to talk to everyone we serve.
>
> In case you didn't know, they call me "ticket-man."
>
> They have called me that for a few years now. A few years of my own metamorphosis from "dude too busy to notice suffering" or "dude too quick to judge who deserves help" to "ticket-man." I hand out tickets so that we make sure we have enough hamburgers for everyone in line. I am no longer "dude who flies first-class to Sydney" or "dude having a drink at the top of the JW Marriott in Hong Kong"; just "ticket-man."
>
> Those who were my age would remember David Byrne chopping lettuce on his arm to "Once in a Lifetime" singing, "You may ask yourself, 'Well, how did I get here?'"
>
> That was me last week on a stinking hot Austin summer day, hugging a homeless guy I did not know wondering, "Well, how did I get here?" Something happens when you serve. Something you cannot control. You start with all sorts of obstacles, fear, incompetence, and even a desire to avoid the hopelessness that occurs when you realize that you do not have the power within you to fix people. Something changes and you stop seeing people and you see a person. Maybe even for a fleeting second you see a person through God's eyes. And you see their heart and they see yours. And you see them see your heart and that is when you get it. Serving was never about them. Serving is about getting gripped in the heart by God. And he touches your heart through the ones you serve. I am not who I was. And it has

nothing to do with anything I did. It is the heart connection to individuals as you serve with no agenda other than telling them, "I see you, you are a person and I accept you for who you are in this moment."

I am ticket-man, and serving has been transformational for me.

Something crazy is happening at ANC. We are a simple church. We teach through Scripture on Sunday, provide a fifth Sunday project for people to serve collectively, and encourage everyone to be in missional community. Yet for those who get involved and take it upon themselves to take it to the next level, their lives are changing.

Men are getting together at 6:00 a.m. to study Scripture. Impromptu women's Bible studies are popping up in living rooms. Teams are being formed to increase awareness and fight human trafficking. People are giving up their time to mentor at-risk kids. Friends are teaming up and engaging the needs of single moms in their neighborhoods. Families are joining forces to walk with the homeless to help them off the streets. Many of our families are adopting or doing foster care. We have people starting nonprofit organizations to serve specific needs in our city. And as their pastor, I rarely know about it until it's already happening or done. All of this is taking place by the initiative of a missional people engaging need the best they know how.

> **Transformation is our goal, not serving for the sake of checking the box of service.**

We all know how to increase our knowledge. We've grown up in a culture that values learning. But when we fail to engage the Spirit and live out what we're learning, we will fail to be transformed. We must come to a new understanding of what it means to be a Christ follower in the Spirit and a new willingness to be on mission together. Transformation is our goal, not serving for the sake of checking the box of service. "Transformation is facilitated by the godly influence of people who understand and integrate their faith and are willing to get involved in the lives of other people."[14]

We have a family who is fairly new to ANC. God took them on a roller-coaster ride after meeting a homeless man and helping him get reconnected with his estranged daughter. They are the perfect example of those willing to "get involved in the lives of other people." While their story is amazing, let me just show you the fruit of their story from part of a recent email.

Serving the least has been so life changing for our family that I can't even begin to tell you all the changes that have transpired. The blessings we have received and are still receiving could only come from God, who is working so presently and powerfully in our lives. If anyone would have told me months ago that our lives were going to be transformed by serving the least of these, I would have never believed it. I am honored that God called us to be his servants. We thank God for entrusting us with this amazing assignment. Our family has seen God's grace, his love like never before, and we wait patiently to where he leads us next.

CHAPTER 7

Embracing the Tension

In chapter 1 I briefly mentioned a pastor friend in Austin who had planned a message series around the idea of engaging need in their community. He had planned for it to be a four-week series culminating with small groups carrying out a once-a-month service project through community. It was a great series. Creative. Thought provoking. And challenging. But somewhere along the way the vision for its being a month-long emphasis was hijacked, and it was reduced to a single sermon. Likewise their monthly service projects were replaced by a one-time missions offering on Sunday.

I have another friend who attends a pretty traditional church in the Dallas area with a pretty traditional mission ministry to match. Similar to my Austin friend, he was in the middle of some pretty heavy tension about his holistic church experience. He wasn't a pastor, but he attended every Sunday, was a discussion leader for a men's Bible study, led an usher team once a month, and hosted a community group at his home. Yet, he still felt as if his faith was shallow. The best way he could describe it was that he was bored with church, and it felt as if what he was a part of was not significant.

He did not feel as if he was growing spiritually, and his ministry efforts were anything but life giving. The good thing was that he was also keenly self-aware that as a consumer he was simply perpetuating the problem. Rarely did he do anything outside of the church walls.

Most of the things he did participate in, he also benefited from. Like many of us, he had a strong urging to do more—not more on the existing church campus, but more out in his community.

In the middle of this tension, it was announced that his church was planning a day of service. He was thrilled to hear that on an upcoming weekend the church was planning to close their doors on a Sunday morning and partner up with others throughout their city to serve those in need. This was way out of the box for them.

On the agenda were twelve projects across the city that he could choose from. People were encouraged to invite neighbors who didn't have a church home. They were encouraged not to simply take the Sunday off, but to make it a day where they could be the church, not just go to church.

Two weeks later, they stopped making the announcement. They never did a sign-up. Never communicated that the event was canceled. The date just came and went like any normal Sunday.

After a little investigation, my friend found out that canceling a Sunday morning service created an amazing amount of backlash. Email after email poured in from members accusing the pastor of compromising the gospel and bending to the "ways of the world." Deacons and elders held special meetings to figure out how to confront the pastor about his reckless leading. Here was their greatest concern: How would they make budget without taking an offering that day?

It was a similar story with my pastor friend in Austin. Everything was fine until small-group leaders found out they had to give up another day of their month to ministry. They were the first to admit they were too busy. Between church, Bible study, soccer practice, and their fantasy baseball draft, they just didn't have the time to add yet another church thing to their calendar.

Both churches canceled their plans, both citing that it was causing too much tension within the church to continue. Just the idea was becoming a divisive force. With so much tension, they surrendered to the thought that God must have not been in it.

It's interesting how much we are willing to work through tension on things we deem worth fighting for. Ladies will spend hours debating the location, somehow navigating hurt feelings and opinions, for next year's Christmas brunch. Leadership teams will meet, pray, and cry for weeks over the theme of vacation Bible school. We'll spend tens of thousands of dollars and just as many hours sitting with a consultant navigating the tension of a building campaign. But the moment we experience tension in serving, we give up and assume God's not in it.

Why is that? Why are we willing to struggle through so much with programming and events, then give up so easily on something that is so clearly mandated by Scripture?

TENSION AND THE SPIRIT

Here's the short and biblical answer to why we have so much tension: "The flesh desires what is contrary to the Spirit, and the Spirit what is contrary to the flesh. They are in conflict with each other" (Galatians 5:17). Whenever there is something powerful on the horizon, something truly of God, we can pretty much expect it to come with or create some tension. It may not even be in us, but it will exist in someone close. In fact, I'm not sure I've ever seen a powerful movement of God that didn't create some type of opposition.

> Whenever there is something powerful on the horizon, something truly of God, we can pretty much expect it to come with or create some tension.

Recently we've had a few dozen families in our church feel the call to adopt or serve orphans through foster care. In fact, it's such a high percentage of people I literally sit back in awe seeing God move. Adoption is a good thing. It's a great thing. Yet God may not call you to adopt. Giving financially to help others who want to adopt but can't afford it is also a good thing. It's also a great thing. However, you may not be able to do that either. Even if you have the means, it's possible that God may not lead you to give. Although no one has ever said a negative word about or to those not adopting, we've had people leave our church because they feel "bad" that they're not adopting.

Tension.

We've experienced the same thing in serving the homeless. Not everyone is drawn to this type of ministry. And for those who don't want to go downtown and feed the homeless, they feel tension when we do go.

We need to make sure we protect our hearts and we search our motives when we start feeling accused or defensive. Before we run out or lash out, we need to take a moment and ask God to search our hearts. And when the opposition comes, we shouldn't be surprised by it; we should be careful not to be scared away too easily. Obstacles are everywhere. As the church, and in our human reasoning, we can easily find a reason not to do just about anything we really need to do.

More often than not, tension serves as a starting point for something in need of change.

More often than not, tension serves as a starting point for something in need of change. It can often expose areas of neglect or concern that never would have been brought to life if left unchallenged. Maybe it's to force us to consider something else we're supposed to be doing. Maybe it's to mentor a kid through Big Brother/Big Sister, to serve a family in need through a local nonprofit, or to take up the fight for clean water in the world through partnering with Charity Water.[1] Whatever it may be, we can be assured that tension has a purpose.

THE ROLE OF TENSION

As a dad with young kids, I've surrendered to the fact that I will not have anything nice, at least not until my kids move out of my house. It takes only a moment for something to be abused, lost, or broken. As a dad, it's a way of life that I've learned to accept.

About a year ago, my eight-year-old decided that he needed to do some pull-ups. The only problem was that he happened to be in the passenger seat of my wife's car and the only thing he could think of to "pull-up" on was the sun visor. As you could imagine, he didn't take the time to think it through, and it didn't go well.

To this day if you were to sit in the passenger seat of my wife's car, you would have a sun visor dangling loosely at about eye level. Your natural response will be to try to push the visor back to its upright position, but you will fail. Yet somehow, you will try again ... and again ... and again. Until someone let's you in on the fact that it's broken and no longer stays put.

The visor does not look like it's broken. It's in perfect form in itself. So it's impossible to anticipate what will happen when you attempt to move it out of the way. While the hook on one side is in perfect condition and keeps it from falling off, the casing on the other side of the visor attaching it to the car is cracked.

This sun visor is held in place by tension. The problem is that the casing that ensures tension is broken. And although I can have it replaced for a few hundred dollars at the Nissan dealership, I choose to let it hang as it may. Without tension, it will not stay in place, neither up nor down. It just flops around somewhere in the middle.

We can rest assured that tension always has a purpose. Whether it holds us in place or just creates a moment where we have to consider our position or check our motives, it always comes with an opportunity for growth. And it can be a great thing for a church needing change. "A congregation that is being led by the Spirit will sometimes experience as much change from interruption, disruption, and surprise as through planning and strategizing."[2]

The problem is that we rarely focus our attention on the right thing. Tension always accompanies an opportunity, a challenge, or a thing to consider. When we place our focus on eliminating the tension, our focus becomes the tension itself instead of the thing we

We can rest assured that tension always has a purpose.

should be considering. This reveals our nature to eliminate the thing causing the tension instead of dealing with much-needed change.

If I were to simply remove the broken casing on my sun visor, I would no longer have a visor on the passenger side of my car. This may be fine when driving at night. But the visor serves a purpose. At certain times, without it, I simply cannot see.

We should not focus on the tension itself that is caused by serving the poor. We should focus on the root of the tension. Is it reasonable? Does it come from a pure place? Does it reveal a bigger problem? Is something broken that needs fixing? If the church were to ask these questions and look for an honest answer, we'd find some life-changing solutions.

TENSION AND LEADERSHIP

Last spring I was invited to sit in on a leadership workshop with about a dozen other pastors. The goal was to brainstorm through some strategies for equipping leaders through creating a model for residencies that could be used in each of our churches. Throughout the day we had the opportunity to introduce ourselves and our ministries, share each of our stories, and present the vision of our church.

Toward the end of the day we were talking about the responsibility given to us through Ephesians 4 to equip the body for works of service. The focus was to brainstorm simple ways to give margin to our people in order to make ministry to the poor a possibility. After sharing the structure of how Austin New Church does this through missional community, one of the pastors looked at me and said, "In order for me to do that, I'd have to blow it all up and start over from scratch."

He was both right and wrong. Right in that in order to do exactly what we do, he would indeed have to start over. We were a church plant that started with a mission-minded DNA from day one. But he's also wrong. There are things he can do and steps he can take to begin to change the trajectory of his church. But that wasn't the important part of what he was saying. Rather, it was the fact that his starting point was not ignorance. He recognized the massive amount of tension that would surround such a major shift in his ministry.

This brings up an important reality about tension: in no place is it felt more than by the people leading the mission. Church leaders not only have to struggle with tension in their own lives and journey; they are also responsible for leading others through the same. The key is in making sure we aren't the ones adding to the tension. We have to help our people recognize their tension and evaluate whether it's from a good or a bad place. Sometimes it's better to help someone see their tension than it is to help them eliminate their tension.

> We have to help our people recognize their tension and evaluate whether it's from a good or a bad place.

TENSION AND GROWTH

Craig Van Gelder draws attention to what he calls a "lens" in which the book of Acts helps us understand the role of tension as a part of the work of the Spirit in the church's life.

> This interpretive lens of growth and development of the church in the book of Acts anticipated the expansion of the church that would continue to take place throughout the ages. In the midst of this growth and development of the church, there are indications that some intentional strategies were used. However, the actual growth and development of the church under the leading of the Spirit was often introduced as a result of conflict, disruption, interruption, and surprise.[3]

We are the church. It makes sense that our personal growth and development would come by the same means. Tension is not a sign of God's absence. In fact, it's the opposite. Tension is most likely the evidence of his presence. Only when we recognize his presence do we grow in his presence.

TENSION AND THE CHURCH

Tension is common in our church culture. It's what we're known for. In fact, how we respond to it is often what keeps people away. With that in mind, it's critical that we come to an understanding of why it's there. There's a huge difference between the wrong motivation and the right motivation for tension.

- The wrong kind of tension occurs when we *protect* what we do. The right kind of tension occurs when we *proclaim* what God does.
- The wrong kind of tension comes when we make it about us and our *kingdom*. The right kind of tension comes when we make it about God and his *kingdom*.
- The wrong kind of tension comes from using Scripture to *defend* our lives. The right kind of tension comes from letting Scripture *define* our lives.

When Jesus sent out the twelve disciples, he let them know to expect massive tension:

> Be on your guard; you will be handed over to the local councils and be flogged in the synagogues. On my account you will be brought before governors and kings as witnesses to them and to the Gentiles. But when they arrest you, do not worry about what to say or how to say it. At that time you will be given what to say, for it will not be you speaking, but the Spirit of your Father speaking through you.
>
> Brother will betray brother to death, and a father his child; children will rebel against their parents and have them put to death. You will be hated by everyone because of me, but the one who stands firm to the end will be saved. When you are persecuted in one place, flee to another. Truly I tell you, you will not finish going through the towns of Israel before the Son of Man comes.
>
> MATTHEW 10:17–23

It's risky to be different in the church. The life of a disciple comes at a cost. A life on mission comes with being misunderstood. Unfortunately believers tend to flog each other in our day. We find it hard to believe that there's not an ulterior motive or hidden agenda when someone makes us uncomfortable.

We have a hard time embracing change or relating. We are suspicious. To be misunderstood by other Christians can be one of the most deflating things about serving the least. We must always guard the line between doing what we do to please ourselves, to please others, or to please Christ. Peter reminds us that, "If you are insulted because of the name of Christ, you are blessed, for the Spirit of glory and of God rests on you" (1 Peter 4:14). When it's the right kind of tension, from the right motivation, we can be sure it's a tension worth living in.

There is a tendency in American Christianity to think we can choose a path without tension. Most of us would prefer to chart our journey that way. But God has called us to join his journey—one that is more amazing, wonderful, scary, awesome, engaging, dangerous, passionate, and rewarding than anything we could ever dream of.

I like how Jeff Vanderstelt, pastor with Soma Communities, put it when he said:

> I'd like to take a more optimistic view of the Spirit. Possibly that the tension does not go away, we don't necessarily get over the hump, but the Spirit changes the way we view tension. We can take pleasure in tension when it comes from "wanting to want to do something good." One of the reasons we need to do it in community ... we're in it together, we can remind each other what is right. We're there for each other in our moment of need, doubt, and struggle. And we find our joy in those relationships.[4]

We don't lead from the safety of the fringe.
We take up residence in the fray.

Where change is happening
Where change is necessary.

There we find ourselves in a unique tug-of-war
between what was, what is, and what could be.

We are faced with the reality
that we are the catalyst in the moment.

A tension ensues between ambitions and fears.

We are tempted to bail on our goals
but discover that under pressure
our vision becomes remarkably crystallized.

A hundred voices attempt to sway us.
And we find we must lean into God with a faith
deeper than we have ever known.

Change happens in the very place where many leaders
flinch, fear, and fail.

The tension we resist is actually by design.
It tests us, it tries us,
It conforms us to His image.

The tension is necessary.
The tension makes us strong.
The tension is good.[5]

CHAPTER 8

Partnering with the
Nonprofit World

My friend Susan was not unlike many today chasing the American dream. She seemed to "have it all" with a successful sales career, earning in the top 10 percent of women in the United States. At first glance you would have never known that she hated waking up and going to work every day.

Like many, Susan casually checked the box of Sunday church attendance, all the while keeping her faith life and church life at a safe distance from one another. Church for her was important, but it never seemed to make the jump from a place you go to sit among strangers to a community of faith to do life with.

At the end of 2009, with the hopes of adding some significance to her life, Susan and a handful of friends decided as their New Year's resolution that they would be intentional about serving those in need once a month. With all the networks and relationships they had made over the years, they knew if they did something worthwhile, many were likely to join them.

In January the group decided to start doing room makeovers at a battered women and children's shelter. They started their service with thirty volunteers, and over the course of the first two months they had remodeled every room in the shelter. By March the word had spread about what these "everyday" people were doing, and the story began to grow. Emails were forwarded, projects were chosen, and teams were filled with volunteers wanting to join in on the "giving back" crusade. That month they served a family of five children who were left to their grandmother after their mother had died in a tragic car accident. Within three months, this humbled group of thirty reached an astonishing five hundred volunteers. The group now has over eight hundred volunteers involved.

After seeing such a void in her community for something like this and realizing she could be a part of filling it, Susan quit her job to take on the task of forming the "Austin Angels" as an official nonprofit organization. Their goal was to choose one "need" project, event, or cause a month and pool their human resources to provide as much support as possible, many times partnering with other local nonprofit organizations.

I first met Susan through Chris Marlow, who runs another nonprofit in town called HELP (Help End Local Poverty). Their two organizations had decided to join forces that month with yet another nonprofit, Communities in Schools. Each year CIS sponsors drives for supplies throughout the city for underresourced schools. Chris had posted on Twitter that they were short some backpacks in order to meet their goal. We just happened to have taken in a large number of backpacks from a donor, and I was quick to let them know they were available.

A few hours later, I met Susan at ANC to hand over a few hundred backpacks.

It was enough to sponsor an entire elementary school. It didn't take long for me to realize that the Austin Angels were doing exactly what we hoped to do in serving our community. I was astonished by the momentum they had in such a short time and was reminded how uniquely positioned a "nonfaith-based" nonprofit was to empower such a diverse group of people to serve.

It didn't take long for me to realize that the Austin Angels were doing exactly what we hoped to do in serving our community.

A few weeks later, I was pleasantly surprised to see Susan and a handful of her friends arriving on a Sunday morning at ANC. In Susan's own words, "The moment we walked through the doors we knew we were home."

Later that year, the Austin Angels joined ANC in partnership along with "Music for the City" and "Restore Austin" to plan an event called Restore the Innocent in order to increase awareness of human trafficking. It was the beginning of another beautiful relationship between Austin New Church and others already doing amazing things in our city.

A handful of the local Angels now call ANC their church home. Each is connected and serves regularly with an ANC Restore Community. Each month their "Serve Your City" event is the current Austin Angels project. Perfect if you ask me. In an email, Susan shared with me, "I have never felt more at home with what I believe in. For the first time I have found a church where faith is put into action."

Almost every one of my nonprofit friends has a story like Susan's. They saw a need and, without the restraints of anything organized, created their own organization to meet the need. Not to be some kind of nonprofit renegade but to do it the way they dreamed. From the ground up, they give everything they've got to make a difference.

There's something to be learned from our nonfaith-based nonprofit partners. Some are secular because they do not have faith. But many choose to be nonfaith-based because they realize the hurdles they have to jump through to get people involved in faith-based initiatives. This is clearly the result of the baggage the church holds today.

We must take seriously our relationships as we form the structures of our church. If church "does what it is" and we hope to be missional, we cannot ignore preexisting organizations and their efforts in our context.

A missional ecclesiology takes seriously the organizational life of the church both in its expressions of local missional congregations and paralocal missional structures. Developing such an ecclesiology in North America will require a careful evaluation of the diverse paralocal organizations that now exist, and how they fit into a more holistic understanding of the biblical character of missional structures generally.[1]

We've found a lot of life in balancing the scale between partnering with faith-based and nonfaith-based organizations. But we don't choose our partners based on whether or not they are faith-oriented in the eyes of the government. Neither type serves as a replacement for the church. Neither is structured as a biblical entity. But both act as service agents for people to make a difference. We choose to partner with such organizations based on what they're doing, how they're doing it, and how effective they are in getting it done.

We choose to partner based on what they're doing, how they're doing it, and how effective they are in getting it done.

The nonfaith-based organization has one major advantage in my mind: unbelievers who serve regularly. We've found it true that "people find a mission that is larger than themselves compelling. They want to change the world. They do not respond in the same way to a church that is sedentary and waiting for the world to come to it."[2] It's a refreshingly new way for skeptics of faith to see Christians when they are serving side-by-side with them. I'm confident it will be good news for them to realize that we serve a God that cares desperately about some of the very things they do.

This hit me when my Restore Community was volunteering for a water station at the LIVEstrong Challenge last year. Literally tens of thousands of people (if not more) gathered on the streets of Austin running, walking, smiling, volunteering, serving, and cheering. We were all gathered in the name of fighting cancer. I'll never forget seeing the mob of runners crest the hill in front of me. They weren't just fighting against a terrible illness. They were fighting for people. Each of us knows someone who has been impacted by cancer. If we were to join the fight, why wouldn't we lock arms with other Christians as well as skeptics, atheists, and agnostics in hope of being hope to each?

Our goal would never be to take Susan out of her sphere of influence and say, "Hey, that Austin Angels thing was great, but now that you go to ANC we want you to use your gifts to oversee this thing we've been working on for the past two years." No way! I'd rather empower her to form community around what she's already doing.

WHY PARTNER?

Several years ago, and prior to planting ANC, I was sitting in a meeting with our senior staff discussing the current state of our church. While we had experienced explosive growth in our first several years of ministry and were still maintaining a pretty advanced growth rate, it was hard not to notice the exodus as well. Each year it seemed the back door was gaining more and more on the front door of our church. And as we sat in conversation about what was happening and how we could stop it, one of our staff made the all-too-obvious statement, "If the common theme of people leaving is that they feel like there's got to be more, then why don't we take a serious look at what they say is missing?"

The search for what is missing has become an all-too-common task of today's church. We're wondering if we're not being creative enough, if our services are too long, if the band needs to play with more energy, or if the greeters aren't making people feel welcome. "Jesus is on people's minds and in their curiosity. They want to be a part of something that is significant ... Being another spectator on Sunday morning is not enough for most people who have not yet found Christ, and it shouldn't be enough for those who have found Him."[3] We naturally take a look at the things we're doing and wonder how we can do them better. Rarely do we take a look at what we're not doing and wonder if we should.

We should see the rise of social concern in the church today as a new opportunity. But we must be careful in relearning how that looks in a community that has thrived for so long without us. We are faced with a unique opportunity not only to reclaim a role in social renewal for the sake of the gospel, but also to do so in a way that increases partnership and promotes some much-needed kingdom-mindedness.

These existing organizations are often a lot farther down the road to serving than we are, and we have a lot to learn from them.

From the beginning, ANC has valued kingdom-minded partnerships. We've recognized that there are others out there who are already taking a stand, already making a difference, and already fighting for some of the same things we want to fight for. And they're doing it well. We've realized that there are people serving regularly throughout our city, and they're doing it just because it seems like the right thing to do. These existing organizations are often a lot farther down the road to serving than we are, and we have a lot to learn from them. There are several no-brainers as to why we choose to partner with nonprofits in our city.

1. Nonprofits typically have a great reputation in the community. As a church we've decided that if we're going to serve our city, we're going to do so in ways that benefit our city, not just us. Nonprofits are typically of the city and for the city. But that's not the reputation of the church. Most people outside the church see our efforts and instantly question our agenda. With that type of reputation we're often limited in what we can do, where we can go, and how much we can get accomplished. While nonprofits are often the most well-connected organizations in the city, churches remain some of the most isolated voices in our community. Nonprofits know city officials and school administrators, are connected to resources, and know who the "go to" people are. What we can spend months spinning our wheels on, a well-connected nonprofit can make happen in days.

2. Nonprofits are experts in their field of work. Rarely does a pastor, staff member, or even layleader have the time or the ability to invest in one task beyond surface level. The result? Ask your best business leaders in your church who have attended a mission trip. Most have been underwhelmed and expect the same next time. On the other hand, nonprofits do what they do, and only what they do. They are the experts on the topic. They know the current legislation and processes. They know the history and culture of the community. They've had years of success, and even more important, they've had years of failure to learn from.

We have a lot to learn from them. The typical project or effort by a local nonprofit offers a better serving experience and often carries a more significant impact on the community. Instead of spending all our time planning the event itself, we can be spending our time cultivating relationships, considering follow-up, and prayerfully seeking gospel-centered movement.

3. Partnering with nonprofits offers a new posture for the church. The church has a reputation of being withdrawn from culture. Whether it's true or not, we're seen as snobby elitists who think we know how best to be a blessing. I'm always amazed when we show up to partner with a nonprofit and see the level of surprise by our colaborers. They simply do not expect to see a church group partner with them. You can almost read their minds, "What's your agenda, bro?" The good news is, they are so used to seeing us do our own thing that when we actually do something outside of ourselves that benefits them, the impact is so much greater.

4. Nonprofit partnership is an easily reproducible strategy. In order to keep gospel-centered missional community central, everything we do is through our Restore Communities—and every community is unique. When we serve primarily through our nonprofit partners, and we have a simple reproducible process, it becomes a plug-and-play process for our Restore Communities—regardless of how many of them we have and regardless of their focus.

For each of our nonprofit partners we ask a simple series of questions: "If you had fifteen to twenty adults serve you, what would they do? How long would you need them? What kind of training goes into it? And what would they need to bring?" We don't tweak the project to fit our need. We do exactly what they ask. Instead of spending all our time as staff planning, promoting, recruiting, and training, we spend our time assimilating opportunities to serve, communicating the process, and empowering our people to go. The nonprofit handles the rest. The best part is that's what they'd hope for us to do anyway. They don't want us with them for our agenda; they just need someone to help them with theirs.

5. Nonprofits need volunteers more often than they need money. Aside from time, the lack of resources is the most common excuse churches make not to serve the poor. It may even be their own fault because of the organizational structure we've created; nevertheless, it is often true. Too often we fail to do something significant because we don't have the budget to make it happen.

While most global nonprofits rely heavily on personal sponsorships and donations, many local nonprofits are resourced through government or private grants. Serving globally is a significant and necessary part of serving the least. That said, serving locally with an already funded organization provides a great opportunity for a church looking for somewhere to start. These nonprofits have warehouses filled with donated supplies. They have staff designed to make sure that your volunteers are coordinated well and that everyone has enough worthwhile stuff to do. While they'd certainly appreciate a financial donation, a working relationship does not hinge on it; often their greatest need is people.

True, there is a lot of crossover. Plenty of local nonprofits need funding, and global organizations still need people. But my hope here is to remind us that a lack of money should never stand in our way. There are plenty of opportunities to start without first shelling out cash.

6. Nonprofits have more non-Christians involved than Christians. For many unbelievers, the nonprofit organization has become their church. Serving with nonprofits has proven to be one of the most significant ways for our people to serve shoulder to shoulder with those far from Christ. And we are there, not because they are our project, but because we're serving together on a project. All kinds of barriers come down when that happens. With that in mind, we often try to serve at projects where we know there will be other volunteers from the community as well.

7. Serving with nonprofits provides a platform to serve selflessly. The church rarely serves selflessly. We can often find a benefit in one way or another from our service. Whether it's a hope that someone will come to our church, a building that is painted that we actually meet in, or a public acknowledgment for what we've done, we love our kudos. At ANC, when we tell our people to do whatever someone else needs us to do, we do the sweating, and they get the credit; that changes things. When we do extreme classroom makeovers with Communities in Schools, neither the teachers nor the principals know it was ANC who did it. They give credit to CIS. And we are helping to empower CIS to make more of a long-term impact in that school that lasts long after we're gone. As church leaders, we need to spend more time figuring out ways to get our people serving, but to get them serving selflessly.

NEW PARTNERSHIPS

There's a lot of baggage that exists between the nonprofit world and the church. Nonprofits have been burned before, and they are gun-shy. One guy promises no agenda, just service, and then the other guy is secretly handing out tracts or taking prayer requests in the corner. It's a gospel-centered bait and switch. We've seen non-profits lose a lot of credibility with those they serve because of an insensitive Christian with an agenda.

We do this sometimes unknowingly. We may have the best of intentions, but we often let our pride get the best of us. We feel noble that we're finally off the sofa and in the streets. We come with the posture that literally screams, "Hey, we're a church, and now we're going to solve all your problems." We treat people like projects. We're condescending. And we're doing anything but making things better for the organization we're trying to serve or the next church trying to make a difference.

How we approach developing a new partnership might be the most important part of the process. Matthew Hansen is the cofounder of ANC's nonprofit branch called Restore Austin and focuses most of his time developing relationships with nonprofits in our city. Through these relationships our hope is to create conduits for service, helping to expose people to real issues of poverty and oppression. Much of what we have done in our city is the result of what Matthew considers the six steps to effective partnerships.

1. Start with a common redemptive purpose. When Jesus sent out the seventy in Luke 10, he told them to look for "a man of peace" (Luke 10:6 NASB). We often read this as, "Look for other Christians." We have to remember that this command was given while Jesus was still alive, meaning at best, there were only seventy "Christians." The "men of peace" were not followers of Christ. Rather, these were probably influential men who shared much of the same values of this new kingdom that was being proclaimed. It was through partnering with these men of peace that the towns to which the disciples traveled would get to hear about this new kingdom. In short, from the beginning of Christ's sending his disciples, he was using partnerships between non-Christians and Christians for his redemptive purposes.

When we look at our world today through the lens of the gospel, we see a God whose heart is broken for the AIDS victim, the orphan, the enslaved, and the oppressed, and we find nothing in the Scriptures that tells us we should only partner with other Christian organizations to serve them. In fact, if we understand the idea of the man of peace correctly, in order to love and serve the broken and oppressed of our city and world, we need to find other nonprofits in our city who have similar redemptive purposes. The one thing that qualifies a nonprofit for partnership is not whether it's a Christian organization, but rather whether they are serving the least of these, much like the church should be.

2. Prioritize developing relationships. While step 1 sounds good, and it is, you will run into differences partnering with nonfaith- as well as faith-based nonprofits when worldviews collide. From church to church we vary in our beliefs. From denomination to denomination we vary. Most certainly from the Christian world to the unbelieving world there will be some huge gaps. The remedy for this is simply relationships. It is not enough to just do work for a nonprofit; rather, it is worth the effort to begin to build relationships with key leaders in the nonprofit you wish to work with. A solid nonagenda-oriented relationship will take you beyond any worldview difference you may run into.

3. Trust their leadership. If you've found that you can't trust their leadership, then move on to a different nonprofit. Don't try to question or change what they do. We have to trust that their wheel has already been invented, and our changing things will only complicate things. We often spend too much time trying to invent something that is already working. The point is not coming up with our own deal in order to take credit. As the church, we are to lead people into a kingdom life. The best way to do this is to allow them to enter into environments of service as easily as possible. We need to jump on board with what is already happening so that the people we are leading have the greatest opportunity to spend their time actually serving.

4. Lose your agenda. All too often the church walks into a situation or partnership with an agenda. You have to remember that you are coming to serve their agenda, and you can do this because you have "shared redemptive purposes" (see step 1).

5. Give away the credit. This is not about you. This is not about the nonprofit. This is about the opportunity to serve those about whom Jesus is deeply concerned — the oppressed, broken, and poor. If you are willing to partner with local nonprofits who have spent years building credibility in different areas of service, take a backseat, and don't seek a name through this. Be willing to follow them. Trust that God has partnered you with them and humbly allow them to lead you as you serve their cause.

6. Commit to be available. There is nothing that builds credibility like being on call for what you claim to believe in. There is a stigma with nonfaith-based nonprofits that the church is only willing to serve on their time, with their agenda, and with their specs. We begin to tangibly deconstruct the view of the church held by nonfaith-based organizations when we are willing to be on call to the redemptive purposes we claim to believe in. Do this long enough, and your local nonprofits begin to lean on you and your ability to mobilize and lead, and before you know it, you become the go-to organization for those in need.

We have followed these steps over and over and over. God has given us credibility, and through that, we have seen AIDS patients come to faith right before their death. We have seen homeless become self-sustainable. We have seen homes built for the homeless, prostitutes, and those who have lost hope. We have seen hope restored, and ultimately God is glorified.

MAKING YOUR PRESENCE KNOWN

In order to develop the best process for partnering in our city, we must make the effort to know our community. Although there are more nonprofit organizations in Austin than any other city in North America, it was important for us to know that they were pretty resistant to and skeptical of the church. Although I believe the redemptive gift of our city is mercy, we still have to deal with the baggage of skeptics before they'll receive mercy from us or offer mercy alongside of us.

While not necessary in every context, we decided it would be helpful to develop an umbrella organization at ANC called Restore Austin. We're certainly not ashamed to let people know that we are a church. But we've found that nonprofits are more likely to partner with us when we communicate from the beginning that we're not going to try to "church it all up." I've been around Christians my whole life. That is not an unreasonable fear. The name also gives a little more vision for what we're about. And no one seems to be confused as to whether or not they can be involved if they don't go to our church. Individuals are more likely to come and serve with us under a more inclusive name. And our people seem more likely to invite, talk about, and spread the word about being part of an organization like Restore Austin.

Restore Austin seeks to create both formal and informal partnerships with other nonprofits throughout our city, acting as a conduit for connecting volunteers with opportunities to serve. Honestly, at first we were a little nervous about partnering with "out of the box" organizations that were atypical for churches. But the more we've stepped out, the more we've realized how diverse the needs are in our city and how diverse the interest is in serving. With that in mind, we've tried to provide as many options as possible in creating a variety of service opportunities for each of our Restore Communities.

Here are a few examples.

Care Communities. Care Communities connect groups of twelve to twenty providing practical and compassionate support to those living with AIDS or cancer in the Austin area. Groups may be asked to do anything: yard work, general maintenance, house cleaning, grocery shopping—depending on each family's need. ANC Restore Communities serving as a Care Community alternate between families, serving a couple of hours per week, as a part of a long-term commitment with each family.

Austin Angels. Austin Angels is a nonprofit organization formed by Austin locals with the desire to give back to their community. Austin Angels partner monthly with other nonprofits and need-based opportunities to mobilize the people of Austin in a collective effort. ANC Restore Communities serve on a monthly basis with the Austin Angels.

Communities In Schools (CIS). CIS is the largest dropout prevention organization in the United States. For more than thirty years, CIS has remained focused on helping kids stay in school and prepare for life by identifying and addressing the unmet needs of children and families. CIS provides a comprehensive solution to the issues that place young people in jeopardy of dropping out. Rather than duplicating services or competing with other youth-serving organizations or agencies, CIS identifies and mobilizes existing community resources and fosters cooperative partnerships for the benefit of students and families. ANC Restore Communities serve weekly through mentoring, quarterly through doing extreme classroom makeovers, and occasionally through seasonal events like backpack drives and holiday sponsorships.

Mobile Loaves and Fishes (MLF). Mobile Loaves and Fishes is a social outreach ministry for the homeless and indigent working poor. Their mission is to provide food, clothing, and dignity to those in need. They accomplish this mission through the use of catering trucks that go out into the city streets of Austin every single night of the week. ANC Restore Communities serve regularly with MLF.

Keep Austin Beautiful (KAB). KAB hopes to inspire and educate individuals and smaller communities toward greater creation stewardship. Their goal is to clean, beautify, and protect the Austin environment through physical improvements and hands-on education. In order to do this, KAB's focus is on litter prevention and litter cleanup, beautification, community improvement, waste reduction, and resource conservation. ANC Restore Communities can either adopt an area to do regular maintenance or serve quarterly for Serve Austin Sunday projects.

Caring Family Network (CFN). CFN provides training and assistance through the process of Fostering to Adopt, provides state certification for Respite Care, and puts on seasonal events for the foster families they serve. Trained ANC Restore Communities and individuals serve regularly with CFN in serving all aspects of the foster care network.

Foundation for the Homeless. Foundation for the Homeless is committed to helping homeless families who want to become self-sustainable by providing housing and life skills as they transition off the streets. ANC Restore Communities serve the foundation quarterly through cleanup, landscaping, and general maintenance on the homes and monthly through sponsoring birthday parties for homeless children.

Capital Area Food Bank (CAFB). The Capital Area Food Bank of Texas provides food and grocery products to more than 350 partner agencies in twenty-one central Texas counties. In 2009, CAFB provided more than 23 million pounds of food. Volunteers are essential to the Food Bank. Each month, volunteers contribute more than 5,000 hours combined to support the Food Bank's mission. ANC Restore Communities help through volunteering in product recovery, at special events, in teaching classes, as ambassadors, and in a variety of other opportunities.

Help End Local Poverty (Haiti). HELP is a global nonprofit organization based out of Austin dedicated to ending extreme poverty by rescuing orphans, restoring their hope, and renewing their communities. ANC partners with HELP to help create sustainable holistic environments in areas of emotional support, health care, economy, and spirituality. ANC Restore Communities serve through quarterly awareness and fundraising events as well as individual child sponsorships.

Eden Reforestation Projects (Africa). Eden does more than plant tens of millions of trees each year. Eden invests in communities through local education, community development, and providing thousands of jobs for the indigenous people of Africa. ANC Restore Communities serve Eden through individual sponsorships and attending vision and ministry trips to Ethiopia.

The Miracle Foundation (India). Millions of children in India share a similar story: a life of poverty with no family and little hope. The Miracle Foundation provides these orphans with food, water, clothing, shelter, education, medical care, love, and most of all, hope. ANC Restore Communities serve The Miracle Foundation through individual sponsorships and attending vision and ministry trips to India.

Nueva Esperanza Orphanage (Mexico). Austin New Church has a working partnership with Nueva Esperanza Orphanage in Mier, Mexico. ANC Restore Communities and individuals have taken several trips to make necessary improvements and repairs on their campus. ANC allocates a portion of our monthly giving to assist with costs of the kids' education, uniforms, food, and other basic needs.

SUCCESSFUL PARTNERSHIP

Recently we received the following email from the volunteer coordinator at one of our major nonprofit partners. In it she expresses some frustration with the church in general, but offers hope for those taking a different posture. Although ANC was named their volunteer organization of the year last year, in my opinion, this email is the greatest reward they could ever give us.

> Hi Matthew and Brandon.
>
> I wanted to say that we have been truly blessed by your service to our agency. You reach not only the students and families we serve but you encourage and serve our staff (myself included) as well. Prior to your involvement with our organization I had been pretty discouraged by the unwillingness of so many churches and believers to partner with the secular nonprofit world or respond at all to the needs of the Austin community. I went back to the outreach table in the corner of the room and was so delighted to see all the ways you are serving people and agencies in Austin. Thank you and I hope that you and the rest of the folks from Austin New Church keep responding to God's nudging because he is speaking through you.
>
> I hope you can see the many victories in this email. I hope you can see the issues that were addressed. And I hope it encourages you to partner more and more as you keep your eyes on the kingdom.

Matt Thomas, bishop for the Free Methodist Church of North America, shared from the Commission on Leadership Development some thoughts on the posture of the church and the role of partnership and collaboration. I agree with every word and am thrilled to see such leadership at the highest level:

> In our present world, the "new Christian" and "un-Christian" alike are not interested in small vision, small scope or internally focused Christianity. Provincialism and colonialism are out. They should be. Partnership and collaboration are in. They

should be. Aware of this, it is significantly important that we identify, partner and celebrate with those who are moving in the right direction, whether or not they fit in our conventional, denominational box or the grist of our theological tradition in its narrowest forms.

By collaboration and partnership, we need to see that we are not functionally or structurally prepared to do everything that needs to be done in the world. But, we can grow in our contribution and partner with those who are functionally and structurally prepared to do great work. In time, we will then not only be contributors to partnerships, but leaders in developing partnerships with other denominations and Christian groups around the world.[4]

CHAPTER 9

A New Metric for Success

This summer my eight-year-old discovered a new love for fishing. Any given day you'd find him ankle deep in mud at the local pond with a pole, a worm, and a prayer. It's amazing how much time he would spend out in the heat staring at a bobber floating across the water. And it was fun watching him discover unconventional ways in trying to catch a fish without ever having to touch a worm.

While he was smitten with the idea of catching a fish, he had developed a pretty serious resistance to both putting on the bait and touching the fish. In the angler world, this is a problem.

So he developed new strategies for fishing when I wasn't there to help. Often this meant combining tackle not designed to go together and usually ended with a knotted mess of fishing line. When I'd get home for the day, I could always tell he went fishing by the presence of his mud-layered fishing pole sitting on the front porch needing to be restrung. I was bailing him out constantly.

One Saturday morning we were fishing, going through the regular routine. I baited the hook and I threw out the line for him. When a fish bit, I set the hook and handed the pole to him, he reeled it in, and then I removed the hook from the fish's mouth.

The next time I tried to let him do it. But I still ended up rebaiting the hook, throwing out the line again, helping him set the hook, and handing him the pole so he could reel in the fish. After watching him stumble for about five minutes, he asked me to remove the hook from the fish's mouth. We did this all morning.

My line never hit the water.

When we got home, Jen asked how we did. With a grin on his face he proudly reported that he had caught eight fish and that Dad had caught exactly zero. Noticing the strange face I was suddenly making, he turned to me and said, "That's okay, Dad, you'll catch a fish someday."

Our perception is our reality. You've probably heard that before. However, our perceived reality is not always the truth. We perceive through the lens of biasness, woundedness, insecurity, selfishness, and an inflated opinion of ourselves.

We know that nothing valuable in ministry happens without God's movement, that our ability is through the Spirit, and that we're called by his grace. He orchestrates movement, provides resources, and crosses our paths with other people. He overcomes our inadequacies, enables and empowers us to respond to their need, and yet we often claim the glory.

> **Success should first and foremost be determined by who gets the glory for spiritual movement.**

Glory cannot be shared. Either we get it or God gets it. Success should first and foremost be determined by who gets the glory for spiritual movement. Too often we give credit to a program, hard work, or creative insight and chalk up every unexplainable victory to good leadership. There are some glaring faults to this logic. And it exposes a real deficiency in the way we view both ourselves and the church.

GIVING CREDIT

We must learn to view success as God views success. Since his ways are higher than our ways, only then will we truly give him credit. Until then we keep it, and it has no eternal value. We may say we do what we do to his glory, but if we're not doing what the Bible says to do, it's still about us.

Jesus taught that every ounce of value found in obedience, sacrifice, and discipline hangs on the command to love God and to love our neighbor (Matthew 22:39 – 40). It only makes sense to consider success through the eyes of both. We fall short personally when our pursuit is to be "first" among our Christian onlookers. Organizationally, we fall short by our internal focus and neglect of those on the outside. How can we love our neighbor and neglect the very things tied to how they perceive us? If we were to truly view success by our faithfulness to Jesus' command to live to put others first, it would change our posture to the outside world.

> We may say we do what we do to his glory, but if we're not doing what the Bible says to do, it's still about us.

Reggie McNeil reminds us in his book *Missional Renaissance* that externally focused leaders must take their cues from the needs and opportunities of their environment. We have to care what's going on outside the walls of our church. We must always look for ways to bless and serve our communities. In order to shift our focus, we must shift much of our calendar, resources, and energy to people who are not already a part of our church.[1]

If we're going to become good news to a broken world, we have to change the way we are viewed by the world. We have to care more about how we measure up to our onlookers than we do our peers. We have to become more externally focused by changing the scorecard based on our impact in the world, not the survivability of our various church forms. "No strategy, tactics, or clever marketing campaign could ever clear away the smokescreen that surrounds Christianity in today's culture. The perception of outsiders will change only when Christians strive to represent the heart of God in every relationship and situation."[2]

In terms of traditional success, serving the least may not improve the bottom line of our organization. In fact, attendance often decreases when we release people for mission. The problem is that many church leaders have spent their entire leadership lives in pursuit of building organizations that rise to the apex of church industry standards. "Changing values and motivations is not easy, but nothing less will accomplish this shift."[3] We will not make the shift from an internal focus to an external focus unless we are willing to change the way we view success. We cannot shift the way we do church without shifting the way we view church.

MEASURING UP

The desire to measure up to our contemporaries is rooted deep in our leadership culture. It's amazing how much a highly attended Sunday can make us feel like the greatest leader who ever lived and how much a lowly attended Sunday can make us question our calling to ministry.

Serving the least is not a fast track to massive church growth. It's not glamorous, clean, or sexy. It's always more messy than expected, requires more time than you hoped to give, and costs more than you have. It can easily lead to a type of church or ministry that, according to traditional standards, could be viewed as anything but successful.

Last summer I ran into a friend who had planted a church a few years prior to our starting ANC. He's a great teacher and does his "style" of church well, and his church has grown pretty rapidly. He didn't know how much my philosophy of ministry had shifted over the past few years. In fact, if he knew some of the priorities I now hold, he might have thought I'd gone a little crazy.

We chatted for a while, talking about all the common topics of church planting. He brought up their new building, their next message series, and how well their youth group was going. Then he went there...

"So how many are you running on Sunday?"

I wanted to vomit. First, because it was a reminder of something I used to value at unhealthy levels. Second, and probably more revealing, part of me wanted to lie to him with the hopes of saving face. Please hear my heart. I don't want to care. But I knew our bottom line would not impress him. What bugged me most was that I wanted to make excuses to maintain credibility in his eyes. That moment revealed that I still have a lot to learn.

ATTENDANCE

There is a refreshing shift in our leadership culture that is beginning to value church growth differently than in the past. I'm a part of a network of church planters called the Austin Area PlantR Network.[4] We meet monthly at the Austin Baptist Association office for a time of networking, encouragement, equipping, and vision casting. And it's funny, almost odd, that you'll rarely hear anyone ask about attendance. It's become such a cliché question, and it comes with many variables and assumptions. Without context, it's really an unfair question.

At first it felt like the elephant in the room. But as time has passed, you can literally sense that the culture has shifted around us, changing our social norm. We give each other permission to value the things we see Christ value. We speak more of mission, transformed lives, and reaching those who claimed they would never darken the doors of a church. We talk about the gospel and kingdom. We strategize ways to partner together and to learn from each other.

> **Measuring success through the lens of the kingdom is life giving. Measuring success by focusing on attendance is like a dog chasing his tail.**

When we orient our ministry around church attendance, we tend to get either defensive and insecure or puffed up and prideful. When we orient our ministry around mission and the kingdom, we tend to get increasingly more dependent on God and increasingly more thankful for his movement. Measuring success through the lens of the kingdom is life giving. Measuring success by focusing on attendance is like a dog chasing his tail. We get tunnel vision, we never arrive, and it will literally drain the life right out of us.

CHURCH GROWTH AND KINGDOM

A Barefoot Church gives priority to the journey over the arrival. It recognizes that people are scattered along the ditch of life. And if we're not intentional, we'll be so distracted by our own agendas that we won't even notice they're there, which neglects the very reason Jesus came.

We live in a church culture where we can easily search, focus, and fight for tangible results regardless of how we get there—many times at the expense of running through people, around our culture, and in spite of greater needs. This stands in direct opposition to what Jesus revealed as his plan for the church: how it would grow and where our responsibility lies. If we're honestly seeking to reorient our life and ministry around the imperatives of Scripture, we have to learn to reorient the way we view church growth as well.

> And I tell you that you are Peter, and on this rock I will build my church, and the gates of Hades will not overcome it. I will give you the keys of the kingdom of heaven; whatever you bind on earth will be bound in heaven, and whatever you loose on earth will be loosed in heaven.
>
> MATTHEW 16:18–19

This is the first moment in Scripture we find Jesus speaking about his bride, the church. He clearly lays out the destiny of the church to overcome the gates of hell. Without confusion he communicates that a successful church would be one that he himself builds. And while it would be built on the revelation of God and faithfulness of disciples like Peter, Jesus was clear that growing the church was to be his focus, not his followers (Matthew 16:17).

Jesus commissioned Peter to take a broader view of success. According to Scripture, Peter's marching orders were literally to discover and unlock the kingdom. As Jesus built his church, Peter's role was to find the things of eternal significance and loosen them—to take the keys and unlock them, knowing that the things we bind will be bound eternally. And the things we loosen will be loosed eternally.

It's not a coincidence today that we struggle so much with letting things go. We hold on to our ways, we hold on to our credibility, we hold on to our reputation. And why wouldn't we? By the world's standards and the desire of our flesh, our identities are often formed and defined by them.

Jesus never gave us the keys to the church. He gave us the keys to the kingdom.

Jesus never gave us the keys to the church. He gave us the keys to the kingdom. When we measure success in church and faith, it must be done by the standards of his kingdom, not our kingdom. If we don't, we're not measuring according to Scripture. This is easier said than done and is an issue of surrendering ownership as much as it is achieving a goal.

OWNERSHIP

Technically, my son can take credit for the fish "we" caught that Saturday morning. He wouldn't be lying in doing so. We were using his pole. He reeled them in by his own strength. We were there on his agenda. And honestly, the day wasn't about the fish, the day was about him. I was glad to let him take credit (kinda).

That's where we miss the boat. We think it's about us. It's not. It's about the Father. Likewise, we wrongly come to the conclusion that it's "our" church. As leaders who've been commissioned to lead it, we intuitively take glory when it goes well. If we're members, we've invested, we've sacrificed, we've been there for "x" amount of years, and we've led this program or sat on that committee, and so we do the same. But none of those things relinquishes ownership. The church is not ours; it never was. We're not owners; we're only stewards. We will never value the things God values until we give back what is already his.

The church is not ours; it never was. We're not owners; we're only stewards.

Paul deals with the idea of ownership in his letter to believers in Rome. At the end of chapter 11, he led them to a deeper understanding of all God had done and who he was. He reminded them of God's mercy and the depths of his riches, wisdom, and knowledge. He referenced how unsearchable his judgments were and marveled at the depths of his mind. Then he closed with a telling statement: "For from him and through him and for him are all things" (Romans 11:36).

Then he continues with our appropriate response:

> Therefore, I urge you, brothers and sisters, in view of God's mercy, to *offer* your bodies as a living sacrifice, holy and pleasing to God — this is your true and proper worship. Do not conform to the pattern of this world, but be transformed by the *renewing* of your mind. *Then you will be able to test and approve* what God's will is — his good, pleasing and perfect will.
>
> ROMANS 12:1 – 2 (EMPHASIS ADDED)

Paul reminds us that everything came into existence because of God; therefore all our efforts, all successes, all things are due him. He continues the theme in chapter 12 by telling us our next steps. In light of this truth we should offer everything about ourselves back to God. To "offer" means to literally relinquish ownership, as when we give a gift. Not only does this please God, not only is this our duty of worship, but it's our proper response.

Paul then says we will be transformed by the renewing of our minds. To "renew" our minds simply means to make new or to change our mind. As Christians, if we were to take the time to consider seriously our inability in light of God's ability, we would see things differently. Our minds would be made new. We would see things in a new way — a different way; more specifically, we would see things differently from how the world sees things.

When we do this, everything will change. The glory will be his, and his kingdom will break through. But don't miss this: the benefit is ours. The fruit of this exchange is that when it happens, we will gain a new perspective from God. We'll gain a new spiritual discernment. We'll gain a new way to view success.

When we hold tightly to our church, our programs, our vision, and our ways, we will always view success as our success. It's only when we surrender ownership of everything that God will see it as a success. Only then will we give him credit in our hearts. And only then will we have the spiritually driven ability to release our desire to succeed in the eyes of the world.

EVALUATING OUR AFFECTIONS

We have an unhealthy affection for things. That's why even a good thing at extreme levels can be bad. Anything can become an idol. That being said, I assure you growth in itself is a good thing. In fact, we should all hope our ministries will continue to expand. It should be our hope. But we should keep careful watch over how much we like it.

As a part of the spiritual formation process at ANC, we spend quite a bit of time talking about tangible ways we can become good news as an intuitive way of life. Last night my Restore Community was having a discussion around the gospel as being good news to broken people. I was incredibly encouraged by all the stories of how members of the group were being intentional about the gospel that very week.

After a time of sharing individual stories, I asked the group to think about how revealing, simple, and powerful each story was, and what it's teaching them about the gospel. Then I asked them to consider what would happen if a group of people collectively gathered around the mission of being good news as a way of life. What would be the impact on our community?

The immediate consensus was that people would want to be involved. That even those resistant to church would be intrigued. And that it would change the way people viewed us as believers.

They were excited to talk about how that might play out. They were being creative in thinking about ways to bridge new relationships with the hopes of making a positive impact on others. They were talking about how the growth would create the opportunity to form new groups and how together the scope of our service could be exponentially larger.

They didn't even realize that we were talking about a biblical model of church where the gospel is central. And they were excited about it growing. They were right in thinking that people would want to be a part of it. Just the idea was refreshing and life giving. Everyone was intrigued. Everyone was smiling. And our affections were on the mission and the relationships, not the numbers.

> If we are in a predominantly unchurched context and our church is not growing, then there is either something wrong or there is something else.

The gospel is not stagnant. It's life giving. Healthy churches grow, but in a myriad of ways. If we are in a predominantly unchurched context and our church is not growing, there's either something wrong or there's something else. Maybe we're not hearing what our culture or community is saying. Maybe we're not structured to do what we hope to do. Maybe our affections or our focus is wrong. Maybe God is withholding growth for a season or for a reason. Maybe God wants us to make a change, do something radical, move us on to the next phase of our life or ministry, or even pioneer a new form of church. Whatever it is, it's worth investigating.

A growing church does not necessarily mean a big church. If you're a church that is constantly planting other churches in your community and sending people into the mission field, you may never be any bigger than you are now.

I have a friend in California who pastors a church of several hundred people. He has the leadership ability and charisma to pastor a church of several thousand. If you were to meet him, you would assume he leads a megachurch. However, over the fifteen years of their existence they have varied between five hundred and eight hundred people in Sunday attendance. During those fifteen years they have planted a dozen or so churches in the same city; the first was planted during their first year of existence.

Every time they grow a couple hundred people, they start a new church and send off a couple hundred people. Most of their daughter churches are now bigger than my friend's church. In fact, if you were to add them all together, they'd be one of the largest churches in America. This is a successful church. Just as well, my friend is an amazingly successful pastor. His affections are on the kingdom, not his kingdom.

NEW FORMS

While our affections can certainly be placed on church attendance in unhealthy ways, I think it's incredible when we see explosive movement or growth in the church. Especially when that growth happens at a church with a kingdom mind-set and a heart to be good news to their community.

Matt Carter pastors a church in Austin called The Austin Stone Community Church.[5] It's an incredible church that has grown at incredible rates. Over the first few years of its life The Stone grew to several thousand in attendance. There were many factors that contributed to their growth. They had a clear calling, vision, and passion for the people and city of Austin, and the presence of God was tangible.

As fast as they grew in their first few years, it was nothing compared to what happened in 2008, the year God presented Matt with the moral imperative to sell out to mission. This included taking the resources they had set aside to build their church campus and instead purchase property in the highest-crime-rate neighborhood of Austin. On it they were to build a city center for mission, leaving their existing church to set up and tear down every Sunday in a local high school gym.

If I were Matt, I wouldn't have slept much. I would have feared everyone would leave my church. I would have feared everyone would think I was crazy. And in my flesh, I probably would have been tempted to figure out a way to do "missional light" instead of "missional."

But The Stone sold out to the mission. They did everything God asked of them to the best of their ability. They sacrificed their new campus, utilized their platform to spread awareness of their new way of church, and reoriented their ministries around a missional posture. I'm sure there were snags along the way that I don't know about. I'm sure there were opportunities lost just as there were opportunities gained. But I also believe they did their best to make each right next decision.

In every form, the moment we seem to have it figured out, God seems to blow up our paradigm.

You might think that a church their size going through such transition would have a season of sifting. Maybe lose some people while enduring a few rebuilding years. But during that year they literally doubled in size. In one year!

I believe The Stone's continued success is about more than just them. I think God's up to something. I think it's a message to all of us that we can trust God's leading and God's ways, regardless our size or style. I think it's a reminder that in a moment where we thought something worked so well, that is when God considered that a new way can be even better. In every form, the moment we seem to have it figured out, God seems to blow up our paradigm. He continuously points us away from shrink-wrapping success and changes the rules.

I don't view church growth in the same way I used to. Much of this change has come through my personal experiences both in serving as a pastor in the megachurch and as a church planter. Some has come through watching God move at The Austin Stone and other churches seeking God's kingdom over their kingdom. Some has come through conversations with proponents of the house church movement experiencing life-transforming breakthroughs. Here's what I've realized: in a city of more than a million people, it's going to take all kinds and sizes of churches filled with people committed to the mission and the kingdom of God. Our success will be a collective success—when God is glorified in our city.

TRANSFORMATION

I've heard it said that the more things change, the more things stay the same. I disagree. The more things change, the more things should change along with it. We should hope for transformed lives, increased hope, life-giving relationships, and for all things to be made new. This is the type of change I desire as a Christian. And honestly, I think it's the type of change the world is looking for.

Change is a good way to measure success. Often change itself is the success. Mostly because it's the work of the Spirit that creates real change. Another way to think about it is transformation. If we were to really evaluate transformation in the church as evidenced by our lives, our relationships, and our joy and peace, it would certainly change what we view as success.

If we were to really evaluate transformation in the church as evidenced by our lives, our relationships, and our joy and peace, it would certainly change what we view as success.

It is not enough to fill our churches; we must transform our world. Society and culture should change if the church has been truly effective. Is the church reaching out and seeing lives changed by the Good News of the Kingdom of God? Surely the numbers of Christians will increase once this happens, but filling seats one day a week is not what the Kingdom is all about. We do Jesus an injustice by reducing His life and ministry to such a sad story as church attendance and membership roles. The measure of the church's influence is found in society — on the streets, not in the pews.[6]

God is moving in the church today in ways that make many of us uncomfortable. Instead of fearing and resisting change, we should consider how God might be in it. At the Exponential Conference in 2009, Craig Groeschel shared the following about change and God's movement:

- God's movement will never be safe, predictable, and clean.
- God's movement will never be about your ministry.
- God's movement will always be about his kingdom.
- God's movement cannot be based on the old measurements of success.

NEW KINDS OF SUCCESS

Success often comes in unlikely forms. For years I've told people going through membership classes that our church might not be for them. For years I secretly hoped that it was. So much so that if anyone were to leave our church, I would inevitably either wonder what was wrong with them, or assume they misunderstood something that was happening.

That's a pretty narrow perspective.

Can it really be a success when people leave our church? Honestly, I've had a few leave that were a pretty big relief. Again, sounds mean. But when we're in the wrong church, sometimes it makes everyone miserable. We meet, we email, we complain, we justify, and we spend countless hours investing in trying to make a fit — and they end up leaving anyway. It's always telling when someone leaves your church and it feels like a relief.

We don't like it when people leave our church. Too easily we feel as if they're leaving us. Like we weren't good enough for them. We get insecure even when it has nothing to do with us or our leadership. We need to learn to celebrate the victories more instead of just mourning the loss. When people leave, we should survey the season we had with them and learn from our time together. This was a hard lesson for me, but I was cured with a single email:

> Brandon,
> Just wanted to ask to take us off your email list. Seems we found a new church as John is needed in the orchestra thru Easter. I guess I will join their choir.

> We really enjoyed your church and you as a minister etc, but my husband really likes to go where he can play in the orchestra. We tried to get him involved at ANC but it didn't happen this time ... oh well. Hope you understand.

It's obvious they were not a fit for our church. They tried their best. But we don't have an orchestra. We also do not have a choir. I'm glad they found a church that did instead of asking us to dig an orchestra pit or buy a portable choir loft.

But my greatest celebration is found in her P.S. It was simply awesome.

> P.S. I have taken clothes down to the ARCH (Advocacy Resource Center for the Homeless) twice now (last week I did a sock drive and took almost 200 pairs + clothes down yesterday with my husband) ... and we found a man who shouldn't be homeless so we will probably be helping him out long term and it's all b/c of your "Hamburger Sundays." Thanks for the nudge to get out and do more for the needy. Blessings.

ANC was not for them. Yet we had an impact on the way they now live their faith. Shouldn't that be the goal of every church? Shouldn't we celebrate when someone leaves to attend another church instead of just leaves the church? This happens all the time. People come. Then people go. I wish everyone could see our church through the same eyes of endearment that I do. But some don't want dancing frogs painted on the back wall of the auditorium. Some would prefer their pastor to not wear flip-flops while preaching. Some don't share our priority in serving. Or perhaps they just want to play in the orchestra.

We talk a good game when it comes to measuring success. We can easily keep track of things that should be important to us but aren't. That doesn't mean we value them. So what are the things that really stretch us? What are the things whose shear ability to count necessitate a new emphasis and priority?

Serving the least is a type of countercultural ministry that should never have become counter to our church culture. But it is. It requires a new way of thinking. While we should certainly make an effort to celebrate salvation, discipleship, and the health of our small groups, let's take a moment to consider some things often neglected in an intentionally out-of-the-box perspective.

Andrew (Hamo) Hamilton shared on his Backyard Missionary blog a post from W. David Phillips, author of *Holy Rewired*, on different ways to measure success. He titled it, *Re-Imagining Success*. "We are prone to measure success by how many and how much. And we determine who is a great leader by how many and how much."[7] He was challenged to provide metaphors that will describe how we measure success in the church in the future. I thought it appropriate to share a few:

1. The number of adoptions people in the church have made
2. The number of classes for special needs children and adults
3. The number of former convicted felons serving in the church
4. The number of calls from community leaders asking the church's advice
5. The number of organizations using the church building
6. The number of emergency finance meetings that take place to reroute money to community ministry
7. The amount of dollars saved by the local schools because the church has painted the walls
8. The number of people serving in the community during the church's normal worship hours
9. The number of nonreligious school professors worshiping with you
10. The number of churches your church planted in a ten-mile radius of your own church[8]

That's a great list. And each point requires us to look from a different perspective than what might come most naturally. Sounds familiar. "But the LORD said to Samuel, 'Do not consider his appearance or his height, for I have rejected him. The LORD does not look at the things people look at. People look at the outward appearance, but the LORD looks at the heart' " (1 Samuel 16:7).

THE INTANGIBLES

I'll admit it. Vince Young has not yet proven to be a great NFL quarterback. But as a Texas Longhorn fan I will die on the hill of claiming he was a *great* college quarterback. He was a man among boys. And when the game was on the line, I'd put the ball in Vince Young's hands over any player in the history of college football.

Yet Vince wasn't what critics called a pure quarterback and his mechanics were often scrutinized. But what he unquestionably had were the "intangibles." The stuff you can't measure on paper. His default mechanism was shear athleticism. And often against the odds, he simply found ways to win.

There are certainly intangibles to faith and church. They are the things you can't nail down and measure, but when the game's on the line, they typically matter more than anything. They are also the things that each one of us must keep an eye on personally. They require some one-on-one time with God, and they are the evidences of the Spirit in our lives.

Without them, there is no way we can claim to be successful, regardless the size of our church, the vastness of our ministry, and the uniqueness of our calling. So here are a few questions to ask concerning the intangibles of our faith journey.

QUESTIONS TO ASK CONCERNING THE INTANGIBLES OF OUR FAITH JOURNEY

Do We Really Love?

One day we'll all stand before God. It will be a day like none other we've ever experienced. I cannot fathom the emotion. I cannot begin to grasp the dimension of understanding that will be new to us. And I cannot imagine the thoughts that will be going through our minds as God speaks his first words to us.

However, somehow I feel as if I can identify a few of the things that he won't say.

- "I was really disappointed with your attendance last Sunday."
- "The problem was that your lobby wasn't big enough."
- "I'm glad you never took a Sabbath. I invented those for the lazy."
- "Wow, you gave waaaaaaaay too much to missions."
- "I wish you would have put more effort into your website. Seriously lame."
- "Yup, you were right all along . . . *poor* was totally a metaphor."

I'm obviously joking about the list. I'm just trying to draw attention to the things that seem to take priority in our lives, the things we worry about that steal our attention and affections, and the things that can become huge distractions to what's really important. Could you imagine for a moment standing before a holy God, who loved the world so much that he gave his only Son, and have him say to us, "I just wish you would have loved others more"?

Jesus told us that there is nothing more important. It's the greatest of all commands to love. There is nothing we can do, achieve, or build that has any value apart from love. Paul put it this way in his letter to the church at Corinth:

> If I speak in the tongues of men or of angels, but do not have love, I am only a resounding gong or a clanging cymbal. If I have the gift of prophecy and can fathom all mysteries and all knowledge, and if I have a faith that can move mountains, but do not have love, I am nothing. If I give all I possess to the poor and give over my body to hardship that I may boast, but do not have love, I gain nothing.
>
> Love is patient, love is kind. It does not envy, it does not boast, it is not proud. It does not dishonor others, it is not

self-seeking, it is not easily angered, it keeps no record of wrongs. Love does not delight in evil but rejoices with the truth. It always protects, always trusts, always hopes, always perseveres...

And now these three remain: faith, hope and love. But the greatest of these is love.

1 CORINTHIANS 13:1–7, 13

There are so many choices to make where faith and real life collide. We feel the pressure to make the right decisions and lead others, often when we have no idea what to do. Here's a suggestion: when in doubt, choose love.

- Can't decide if you should give? Choose love.
- Can't seem to swallow your pride on a foolish matter? Choose love.
- Having a hard time forgiving someone? Choose love.
- Rather keep your time for yourself than help someone in need? Choose love.
- What would Jesus really do? Choose love.

One of the reasons I believe in a Barefoot Church is because I believe in the power of love. Not just as a feeling, but as an action. Jesus was clear that we were to serve the least, and he was clear that it should always be as an act of compassion. Our love should extend toward one another as well. And through that love, people will see God, not us or our actions.

A new command I give you: Love one another. As I have loved you, so you must love one another. By this everyone will know that you are my disciples, if you love one another.

JOHN 13:34–35

Do We Have Peace?

We are doing a study through the book of Romans right now at ANC. It's a pretty challenging study. The topics are so closely connected, and it can get so academic that it can be difficult to keep each week fresh. However, one of the redundant themes of Romans is one that always refreshes: peace with God.

> Therefore, since we have been justified through faith, we have peace with God through our Lord Jesus Christ.
>
> ROMANS 5:1

Peace with God is found to be a favorite theme throughout Paul's writings. In several of his letters to the church he signs off with a hope for peace. He uses it as a blessing, an encouragement, and a reminder of the way of Jesus.

The word "peace" in Romans 5 comes from the word *eiro*, which means "to join" and implies being "set at one again." The doctrine of peace encompasses the idea that we are reconciled back to God through Jesus and are now at peace with him. Once separated. Now back together. Just the idea is refreshing to me.

So few of us live in peace. We have such a desire to prove ourselves that we're constantly striving for the next thing we can do for God. Whether in ministry or life, this can become a chasing after the wind. If God does not require something of us, why do we require it of ourselves? If God considers us at peace with him, then why are we not at peace with ourselves?

Being at peace with God means we can take a breath, relax, and stop performing.

Being at peace with God means we can take a breath, relax, and stop performing. Because of Christ, we don't have to prove ourselves worthy to God. We no longer have to find our identity in the approval of others. And we don't have to be perfect. Jesus took care of that.

Peace is the gift of Jesus and should be a huge part of any believer's success metric. The lack thereof is evidence of upside-down priorities, insecurity, or selfish ambition. Does something bring us strife? We should evaluate whether or not it's of Jesus. Do we have a complete lack of peace? Most likely there's a reason.

Peace I leave with you; my peace I give you. I do not give to you as the world gives. Do not let your hearts be troubled and do not be afraid.

JOHN 14:27

Do We Have Joy?

The most obvious and yet least measurable of all the benefits of the Christian life is joy. Joy is not something we can do or manufacture. Joy is something you have, something you bring to others, something you share, something you respond to, and something you rejoice in. Nehemiah reminds us that "the joy of the LORD is your strength" (Nehemiah 8:10). Not only do we want joy, we need joy. Yet, once again, it's something that so many believers are lacking. And according to recent studies, it's something so many pastors are lacking. If we do not have joy, we're missing something deeply important.

I was floored as I plugged the word "joy" into my Bible search program. Not at the number of times it's mentioned in the Bible, but by where the Scriptures say it comes from. It may appear as if I picked the ones that best make the point of my book, but I didn't. The majority of Scripture reminds us what happens when we have joy, but only a handful of the verses describe how it actually comes. Scripture teaches that we experience joy...

When we trust in our salvation.

"Surely God is my salvation;
   I will trust and not be afraid.
The LORD, the LORD himself, is my strength and
      my defense;
   he has become my salvation."
With joy you will draw water
   from the wells of salvation.

ISAIAH 12:2–3

When the Spirit is present.

At that time Jesus, full of joy through the Holy Spirit, said, "I praise you, Father, Lord of heaven and earth, because you have hidden these things from the wise and learned, and revealed them to little children. Yes, Father, for this is what you were pleased to do."

Luke 10:21

And the disciples were filled with joy and with the Holy Spirit.

Acts 13:52

When justice is present.

> When justice is done, it brings joy to the righteous
> but terror to evildoers.

Proverbs 21:15

When we promote peace.

> Deceit is in the hearts of those who plot evil,
> but those who promote peace have joy.

Proverbs 12:20

When we love.

If you keep my commands, you will remain in my love, just as I have kept my Father's commands and remain in his love. I have told you this so that my joy may be in you and that your joy may be complete. My command is this: Love each other as I have loved you.

John 15:10–12

The Bible clearly links our joy to one of two issues. First is the understanding and resting in our salvation through Christ and the presence of the Holy Spirit. The second is the presence of justice, the promotion of peace, and the existence of love in our lives.

These themes sound remarkably similar to themes of Micah when he wrote what God requires of us: "to act justly and to love mercy and to walk humbly with our God" (Micah 6:8).

We should pray for these things. And we should be faithful to respond to the Spirit's leading in these things. If we take to heart Christ's calling on our lives to a full life (John 10:10), then joy should certainly be a part of the equation. If we do not have joy, we should look deeply into what we are doing and why we are doing it.

Are We Faithful?

I'm amazed that people still come to our church. Although I know there is an increasing desire in our culture to serve the least, I still drive up on a Sunday morning wondering if this will be the day no one shows up. Sometimes I wonder if ANC will scratch the itch for people for a while, then eventually they'll come to their senses and find a church that fits the American dream a little better.

And honestly, that day could come. With the consistently decreasing church attendance across the American landscape, it could come for all of us. It's a possibility that in our lifetime, church as we now know it could cease to exist in its current form. I'm not saying church will disappear; I'm saying that our current forms are certainly being challenged.

I can't help but wonder if the worst-case scenario for each of us were to take place, could we stand before God and claim that we have been faithful to that which we've been called?

The greatest gift that God gave us at ANC was the certainty of our calling. He never told us to try to build a big church. His vision was clear for us to serve the least, invest in his kingdom, and make disciples who do the same, and *he* would build his church. So that's what we've tried to do. And we've been fortunate that the church of our dreams has emerged.

There have been times that our vision has forced us to make some unlikely decisions. We often joke how it seemed as if we were trying to sabotage our church rather than plant one. More than once we've been faced with a difficult leadership decision that appeared to be in opposition to building sustainability or stability. Here are just a few:

- Although we planned to hold our first public gathering on Easter, we felt we should make a different first impression in the community other than a "come to us" event. So we canceled it and channeled all our launch resources into hosting a community-wide food drive.
- The next year while struggling to figure out when to add an additional service for the Easter crowd, we landed on having just one, moving our service outdoors and downtown to have worship and share communion with the homeless community we serve.
- In our first year as a church plant we committed 58 percent of our church's tithes to mission and led over 125 service projects.
- On our one-year anniversary we gave over $20,000 (more than 75 percent of all we had) to an East Austin ministry so they could secure a place to meet in a strategic location.
- During year two, we moved out of our rented multimillion-dollar fine-arts facility into the back room of an old dance academy in a diverse south Austin neighborhood. Although it was cheaper to stay, the fine-arts facility didn't match our vision, and we felt it gave a false first impression to our visitors about who we were.
- Last summer we had emergency board meetings nearly every week to discuss our financial crisis. Yet at the same time we hosted another church plant at ANC, partnered with them for their launch, and encouraged our people who lived in their area of town to leave our church and join them.
- We've completely stripped our church of programs and events to give room for people to live on mission. This has forced us to be creative with just about everything else we try to accomplish as a church.

I remember an email we received from a single mom in our community needing $900 to bail her out of a tough financial situation. We got her request on the same day Tray informed me that we only had $1,200 in the bank. With payroll approaching, it was the lowest point of our church's financial history.

I remember sitting at my breakfast table by Jen, with Tray on the phone, thinking that we just can't do anymore. Trying to convince myself that we've done enough—that we've given and given—and we've finally hit our threshold. And it was okay. We just didn't have it to give this time.

But we did have it to give. She needed $900 and we had $1,200.

I hung up the phone, looked across the table at Jen, and cried. We had to give it. I remember feeling that maybe it had really come to this. That we would give the money away and it was over. Close the doors. Reinvent our structure to survive. Whatever it took we were going to do it. My exact words to Jen were, "If we're gonna go down, we're gonna go down swinging. God didn't call us to withhold from someone in need." So we gave the $900.

The next day we got a $10,000 check in the mail. It was from a private supporter who didn't attend our church and had no idea where we were financially. This has happened four times now, each within twenty-four hours of a massive financial sacrifice, each time an unexpected gift of $10,000.

I know there are leaders and churches that have made much greater sacrifices than these. I'm constantly amazed by the stories I hear. But here's my point: if the doors of our church closed tomorrow, I would consider what we've done a success, and I'd look forward to what was next. Why? Because to the best of our ability, we've been faithful to what God has called us to do. We've used that as the primary barometer in determining our next steps so many times—even when it didn't seem to make sense—and we've seen such direct fruit and ministry in following, that we feel confident we are the church we are supposed to be. If it ended abruptly, we could hold our heads high knowing that God was up to something new.

A friend of mine named Brent has planted a church called The Well. In fact, they're probably even more radical than we are in posturing the church to serve the poor. It's a beautiful faith community filled with people on mission. Three years into the plant, he and his family felt the call to leave The Well for full-time missions in Africa. So they went.

Most church planters could never imagine leaving their church. I share the sentiment. And I would imagine that at one point, Brent had felt the same way. But this certainly didn't mean that his ministry at The Well was in vain. He wasn't bailing on the church. It didn't mean he misheard God when he started it. It just meant that he was still faithful, regardless of where the journey took him.

He and his wife, Leah, now serve as pastors to a village of families and orphans in Uganda who are HIV positive or have full-blown AIDS. An entire village set aside. I believe with all my heart that when we get to heaven, Brent and Leah will be at the front of the line and one of the first to hear, "Well done, my good and faithful servants."

THE TRUTH ABOUT SUCCESS

Let me be transparent for a moment. I think we already know what God values more than we'll admit. Just take whatever is self-serving and do the opposite. Anything that makes the name of Jesus famous is success. Anything bringing us glory is not.

We need to apply some of the same principles to measuring success that we would in characterizing how we grow up as adults. We need to speak truth and stop using self-serving and foolish reasoning. We need to learn to do right, to seek justice, to encourage the oppressed, to defend the cause of the fatherless, to plead the case of the widow, and to become the man or woman God intends us to be (see Isaiah 1:17).

When I was a child, I talked like a child, I thought like a child, I reasoned like a child. When I became a man, I put the ways of childhood behind me.

1 CORINTHIANS 13:11

Ultimately, we must measure all success through the lens of Christ. I hope that's what all the above is about. We have to be champions of his gospel. We have to ask whether or not we are developing a distinctive people of God who are compelling to our city. At the end of it all, what we build will burn up unless it's about Christ.

CHAPTER 10

Becoming a Barefoot Church

Last month I had the opportunity to spend a couple of days with Hugh Halter and Matt Smay of Missio and Bob Logan of CoachNet at the Missio Intensive in Denver. It was a great day of frank discussion and practical discovery. After processing the day, Bob made a fitting point on his blog:

> If we could implement even 20% of the ideas — and this is true of the ideas at most conferences — we'd be miles ahead in the church today. This is why I've been thinking about implementation lately. So many great concepts, but what do we actually DO? And how do we do it? Take an idea — any idea — and ask, "What would that look like? How could we put legs to that idea?"[1]

My hope as you finish this book is that whatever you choose to apply, that it's not what is easiest or most strategic, but what is most Spirit-led. I pray that somehow you've been led through a journey of self-discovery at a soul level. I pray that you've been confronted with tension, the good kind, and that you've allowed the Spirit to sift you through.

I agree with Neil Cole's words from *Church 3.0*:

> Unfortunately, as the world looks at our churches, particularly in the West, it sees only what people have done or what programs

they are doing. The world is not impressed. In response, we scheme and plot and plan: *"What can we do to make our church more appealing to the people in our community?"* This is, once again, the wrong question. It's as if we're trying to boost God's approval ratings. It is God's name that is at risk, not ours, and we are not responsible for protecting His reputation. He can handle that, by Himself, just fine. A better question is, *"Where is Jesus seen at work in our midst?"* Where do we see lives changing, and communities transforming simply by the power of the Gospel?[2]

My prayer is that we discover fully the joy of the gospel and that we give ourselves permission to live in the margins. By now

> **My prayer is that we discover fully the joy of the gospel and that we give ourselves permission to live in the margins.**

you know I believe deeply in the journey to the end of our selves, the place where Jesus is often found, and where God is ultimately glorified. That place is where peace is found. It's where joy is found. Where contentment in our journey is found. As Albert Schweitzer once said, "One thing I know: the only ones among you who will be really happy are those who will have sought and found how to serve."[3]

Alan Hirsch and Dave Ferguson offer a profound yet simple starting point in their book *On the Verge*: "The first responsibility of a leader is to define reality."[4] If we are trying to get somewhere, we must first identify our starting point in relationship to where we want to go. When we are trying to find a particular store in a shopping mall, the first thing we do is locate the directory that displays the floor plan of all the shops. Our eyes immediately land on the red dot with an arrow pointing to it that says, "You are here!" Once we know where we are, we can locate our intended destination and plot the pathway to get there.[5]

In order to give some practical next steps for implementing the concepts of a barefoot life, let's do so by defining our starting point, our contextual reality, and our current church culture.

STARTING POINT

The most frequent question I hear is this one: "Where do I start?" Honestly, it depends. Are you talking about a church? A nonprofit? What's the history (i.e., baggage or success) of the organization in relationship to what you're trying to do? Each answer changes the game plan a bit, as it should. Fortunately, there is no shrink-wrapped plan for engaging need collectively; it takes both thought and effort. This is our backdrop for everything else.

There's a second set of questions: Who are you? What type of authority do you have? Do you have a corporate agenda? What's your role in the organization? Ultimately what I'm asking is, is it your place to make a change? The answers to these questions might give some clarity as to whether this change is to be about you, the organization you want to see changed, or both.

The good news is that anyone at any time can become more socially active. It's a decision of the mind and heart. You can do so at any church, of any size, with any model or structure. The most beautiful part about our journey is that it's our journey, and it must start with a personal response prior to a corporate response. There is always a bigger picture, but our piece of that bigger picture is critical. It's tied to our hearts and minds and has everything to do with our contentment, peace, and joy as we seek to stand blameless before a holy God who is at work in our world. Every Christian has been given the priestly responsibility of being a minister of hope and reconciliation. Whether or not we embrace that calling impacts us; how we embrace it impacts others.

Every Christian has been given the priestly responsibility of being a minister of hope and reconciliation.

For the Layperson

First, go do it yourself. The best you know how. Just do something. Seek out more understanding and seek out simple opportunities. Make care packages with your family for Valentine's Day and hand them out to the homeless, spend a day of volunteering at the local food pantry, sponsor a single mom for Thanksgiving dinner or Christmas, or volunteer at the nursing home. Pray for God to open your eyes to a new level of need and a new level of willingness to do something. I assure you, your eyes will be opened.

Then embrace the journey. I know that sounds simplistic, but that's how it starts. Make each right next decision. Take it one step at a time and be faithful in the moment. Here's a guarantee: it will begin to create tension in your life. But as we discussed earlier, tension is good.

Maybe you're part of a church that embraces service to the poor. If so, set up meetings with the appropriate staff to figure out how you can get more involved. If not, pray for your church and your pastors, and be patient. Share your heart, but don't be annoying. Be considerate for ministries, programs, methods, and values that currently exist. People have poured out their heart into existing ministries, and they believe in them. We simply cannot expect everyone around us to jump right into the journey at the place where we are.

> **We simply cannot expect everyone around us to jump right into the journey at the place where we are.**

Most of us don't know what to do with our tension. It's important that we don't displace our tension onto someone else. Always deal with yourself and your life first. Be willing to be a part of the answer. This is especially true when thinking of our church leaders; we cannot expect everyone else to make the change for us. If our hope is simply to consume whatever new ministry or event they come up with, we've missed the point.

If you don't feel as if you have any type of support in your faith community and you continue to experience roadblock after roadblock, first prayerfully ask God to search your own heart and motive. Ask him to reveal any place you've stepped out of line or have been divisive. If you continue to feel like a fish out of water, find a new church home. It's not your place to lead that church where you want it to go. If it were, God would make you their pastor. Chances are, God already has the pastor on a journey, and he already has a vision for that church and for those people. One day we'll see and understand.

For the Unchurched or Dechurched Christian

Do the same things just mentioned. Do it yourself first. Pray. Be a learner. Be available. Be willing. But you must find a faith community on mission and join them. The church you dream of is out there. It may not look like the church of your dreams (yet), but maybe you're supposed to be a part of its getting there. I can't help but believe this journey is to be shared. This verse from Hebrews comes to mind:

> Let us hold unswervingly to the hope we profess, for he who promised is faithful. And let us consider how we may spur one another on toward love and good deeds, not giving up meeting together, as some are in the habit of doing, but encouraging one another—and all the more as you see the Day approaching.
>
> HEBREWS 10:23–25

For the Associate Pastor or Ministry Director

The most important thing for you to remember is that you are not the lead pastor of your church. You have willingly submitted yourself to the leadership in place. If the vision of your church is to serve and press into issues of mercy and justice, then praise God, go to your pastor, and ask him how he feels you should best utilize your gifts, abilities, and authority to further the cause. However, if the two of you are not on the same page, you should pray for wisdom like you've never prayed before. There are two major dangers for associate pastors and ministry directors who are at a church with a lead pastor who does not hold their passion for social action.

It can become a divisive issue. This is a touchy subject for many. Even if you think you hold the authority to shape your ministry around what we're talking about, it's always best to speak with your lead pastor first. Share your heart and your agenda. Ask for boundaries and permissions. Then honor them. Don't start with asking what your ministry leaders or volunteers think. If they jump on board, yet your pastor has a different vision, it can end up causing unnecessary tension—the bad kind. Even division.

We can miss our calling. Is it possible that God is using this tension to move you into a new season of ministry? We've spoken extensively about holding things "loosely" as followers of Christ. If we feel confident that we are to press into social action but do not hold the authority as a leader to do so, maybe it's time to move on.

If you are resisting this possibility, I'd like you to consider if you're holding your current position too tightly. Start by asking God to reveal the reasons you want to stay. A paycheck, good insurance, your new house, and great schools are not legitimate reasons. However, give your pastor a fair shake first. Who knows, maybe God is moving you within the organization. Maybe your pastor is considering the same, and you might be the voice of reason taking him off center. It's also possible you will lose your job. If you cannot honor what God is calling you toward in your life where you are, this is the best thing that can happen for you. I can't write this part of the journey for you, but I assure you that you know the one who can.

Lead Pastor or Church Planter

There is literally nothing holding you back except you. You have the authority. You have the calling. And you have the gifting and ability to do whatever God is calling you to do. That being said, you should still start at home. Prayerfully involve your wife and family. Prayerfully digest the tension in your own life and ways. As we all know, we cannot lead others where we have not gone ourselves. In regard to your church, you cannot outsource a call to social action; you have to champion it. This is not a new method or strategy; it's applying a biblical truth in a new way, and it must start with you.

THREE NECESSARY STEPS IN MOVING FORWARD PERSONALLY

1. Be convicted. This has to be something that God is putting on your heart for the right reason. If it is not, it will be burdensome to you and your leadership. Start with prayer and end with prayer. Ask the Spirit to show you where you yourself are falling short. You don't even have to know exactly what you're being convicted about, you just have to feel something, know something has to be done, and be willing to do something about it.

2. Be convinced. Settle the issue of theology. Study the Scriptures. Not everyone agrees, so expect conflict; pray and do some more research. One way or another you'll either land on seeing social action as a significant piece of the gospel, or a necessary part of a Christian's life running parallel to the gospel, or something completely unconnected. Two out of three of those demand a response. Without being convinced that you are pressing forward out of biblical mandate or moral imperative, your leadership will lack the power and confidence you need. Those following can see the difference.

3. Be confident. Confidence is the fruit of the first two steps. When the tension comes, you will either forget why you're doing it and bail out or remember God's leading and instruction and fight for it. There will be a time when you'll feel you have to remind God that it was his idea. He already knows that. Do you?

Leading people through change is an art, not a science — especially when leading others toward engaging need for the first time. There are variables, many obstacles, and several paths that can lead to similar outcomes. Each of our stories will be unique, and half of the journey is discovery. Don't limit yourself before you get out of the box.

THREE KEYS TO LEADING OUT-OF-THE-BOX INITIATIVES TOWARD SOCIAL ACTION

1. Be creative. Things will not go as planned. Serving the least is not neat and tidy. We will constantly have to be thinking about how we can accomplish specific things through unconventional means. This minimizes structural change and is necessary in (a) discovering existing forms that can best be adapted to accomplish our new objectives, (b) utilizing individual gifts to succeed in unlikely ways, and

(c) thinking out of the box in an area where we've been conditioned to follow the norm.

2. Be intentional. This is not something that will happen spending six hours a day at Starbucks sipping on a frapaccino. You won't find out what you need to know at your laptop. Prayerfully drive through your community, meet with nonprofit directors and city demographers, read books on culture and community, and meet with your mayor. Nothing we do should be without a purpose. If you plan an event to serve single moms, use the moment to capture information about their greatest needs. If you're talking to a homeless man, ask him what misconceptions most people have about homelessness. If you're mentoring a kid at school, find out if you can serve the mom as well. Being intentional means being a learner again. Know what you're trying to accomplish and steward your efforts accordingly.

3. Be responsive. There's a huge difference between reacting and responding. When things do not go as expected, don't throw up your hands in frustration. Don't give up. And don't allow the enemy to question all the things you've already settled. Be prayerful and find out what the next best decision is; then go do it. I know this seems a little happy-go-lucky, but don't look at things as failures; instead, look at them as opportunities. Find alternatives and be open to changes along the way.

CONTEXT

We live in a post-Christian and postmodern context. This changes the way the church should interact with society, because the way society views the church has certainly changed. Dr. Stuart Murray teaches that "post-Christendom is the culture that emerges as the Christian faith loses coherence within a society that has been definitively shaped by the Christian story and as the institutions that have been developed to express Christian convictions decline in influence."[6]

Murray offers seven significant ecclesiological shifts from Christendom to post-Christendom. It is critical that we understand these in order to view appropriately our place as Christians in a post-Christian society.

- *From the center to the margins.* In Christendom the Christian story and the churches were central, but in post-Christendom these are marginal.
- *From majority to minority.* In Christendom Christians comprised the (often overwhelming) majority, but in post-Christendom we are a minority.
- *From settlers to sojourners.* In Christendom Christians felt at home in a culture shaped by their story, but in post-Christendom we are aliens, exiles, and pilgrims in a culture where we no longer feel at home.
- *From privilege to plurality.* In Christendom Christians enjoyed many privileges, but in post-Christendom we are one community among many in a plural society.
- *From control to witness.* In Christendom churches could exert control over society, but in post-Christendom we exercise influence only through witnessing to our story and its implications.
- *From maintenance to mission.* In Christendom the emphasis was on maintaining a supposedly Christian status quo, but in post-Christendom it is on mission within a contested environment.
- *From institution to movement.* In Christendom churches operated mainly in institutional mode, but in post-Christendom we must become again a Christian movement.[7]

If we are to become missionaries to our culture, we need to take these shifts seriously. If we do not understand how our context impacts our process, we will become less and less relevant, and our voice in our community will continue to decrease. We can no longer hit the streets with the bravado of a traveling evangelist. We must come in humility, in peace, and in love.

CHURCH CULTURE

Starting something new can be challenging. Bringing change to something that's been around for years can be shockingly complicated. Craig Van Gelder does an amazing job of discussing the types of change we encounter in the church. In doing so he encourages us to consider both our current church culture's resistance and complexity of change. "Not all changes introduced into a congregation have the same level of complexity or difficulty associated with them, and not all elicit the same level of resistance."[8]

There are four types of change we need to understand:

1. Improvement. This is introduced in one of two ways. The first way is by the addition of a new initiative where something is being added to a present ministry that was not present before. The second way to make an improvement is to upgrade an aspect of the ministry. "These planned changes do not fundamentally challenge the core values or beliefs of a congregation. While they may encounter some resistance and introduce some pain, these can usually be dealt with in fairly simple ways—practicing good communication, meeting with a few key people or groups, or inviting feedback and suggestions."[9]

2. Adjustment. "An adjustment is a type of planned change that adds another dimension to the process. In this case, a congregation is required to unlearn the way it has been doing something and to relearn a new way to do it."[10] Since this type of change requires two responses from people, letting go of something old and adjusting to something new, this may come with even more resistance but still can be introduced without making any fundamental changes in vision, core values, or beliefs.

3. Revision. This happens when a change is introduced that requires a redirection of ministry or reorientation of the basic vision of a congregation. "Here something in the core identity of the church is being shifted, or some of the core values and beliefs are being challenged and changed."[11] Here a leader must anticipate and plan to proactively engage resistance. Avoiding or ignoring resistance will only prolong the reality. In this situation, Van Gelder recommends

(a) extensive conversation with key leaders and groups most affected by the change, (b) regular opportunities for feedback, and (c) clear communication on why the change is being made.[12]

4. Re-creation. This comes at a time where a congregation may literally have to reinvent itself in order to survive. Their core identity and values may be obsolete. "The process of re-creating is complicated for many congregations because they often resist changing until it is too late. Usually there is a time lag of years between re-creation being required and when those providing leadership in a congregation are able to come to grips with it."[13] Van Gelder reminds us that seldom can a congregation successfully go through a re-creation. If change is inevitable, then the sooner the better.

PHASES OF CHANGE

Change happens in waves. There are low points and there are high points. Just like a wave, there is a cycle of change that repeats itself and builds on itself while moving forward. The type of change you are encountering, your context, and your church culture should all factor into determining how much you "bite off" with each cycle. If you need to go slower because of a deeply ingrained resistance, then each cycle should be more specific and focused. While there are several cycles to change and while the objectives may change each cycle, each phase repeats itself. Objectives must be determined on a case-by-case scenario.

Phase One: Communication
- Communicate a clear and honest picture of where you are now.
- Communicate a convincing case for what you're lacking.
- Communicate a clear plan for where you hope to go and why.

Phase Two: Preparation
- Prepare your congregation with the bigger picture. Be creative.

- Prepare your impacted groups with a vision supporting the big picture. Be clear.
- Prepare your key leaders by equipping them for their new role. Be concise.

Phase Three: Transition
- Transition and keep to the original plan—as much as possible.
- Transition while owning mistakes or misconceptions that force a change of plan.
- Transition by communicating where you are along the way.

Phase Four: Reinforcement
- Reinforce why you're making the changes.
- Reinforce your leaders with encouragement and a platform for evaluation.
- Reinforce your commitment to what the change is about and why it's important.

Phase Five: Recommunicate and repeat
- Revise based on where you are now.
- Recast the vision from your new starting point (celebrating any movement).
- Repeat the phases of communication, preparation, transition, and reinforcement.

MAKING CHANGE A REALITY

This year I'm helping coach my son's peewee tackle football team. With the kids it's been a blast. With the parents, it's been one of the most frustrating things I've ever experienced. Every parent thinks their son should be the starting quarterback. Every parent thinks their kid should play more than they do. And every parent has an excuse for why they can't get their kid to practice yet somehow manage to make every game. Including me. I wish we could take what we now know about the season and call a big fat "redo" on the parent meeting at the beginning of the year. As much as we tried to communicate expectations up front, we simply had no idea what was ahead of us.

It's good when everyone knows what to expect. That doesn't come naturally, especially when making a major change in the way we do church. We need to do everything we can to cultivate a culture of flexibility during change. The best way to do this is to communicate a new type of cultural expectation. The following are four objectives we've found to be critical to introducing social action.

1. *Make it a priority.* In order to create a culture of service, we have to communicate and structure serving as a priority, not an add-on or optional event. We can do this in a number of ways.

   a. *Platform.* The most underutilized platform is Sunday morning. We need to use it not only to preach our sermons but also to cast vision regularly. The mistake we sometimes make is waiting until we have it all figured out before we share. Bringing your congregation in on the journey, possibly even starting with a confession of neglect, can be one of the most powerful ways to lead. This is a great time to proactively address anticipated objections, concerns, or misunderstandings. If we are not willing to utilize our Sunday mornings to regularly communicate serving, it's simply not our priority.

   b. *Prayer.* In addition to serving being an everyday priority, we called our people to a month of prayer last year specifically on how God may be leading them to serve. We closed the month with a week of guided study and a day of fasting. That weekend became one of the most amazing times of commitment we've ever had at ANC. And the ministries that resulted from that season of prayer form some of the very heart of who we are today. We need prayer without change. How much more do we need it while leading others through change?

c. *Scripture.* We would never make a point during a sermon without building a scriptural foundation, yet we tend to expect people to serve just because they should. Share not only from your heart, but also from your Bible. Scripture has plenty to say about serving the least. We can have confidence that the Word will not return void.

d. *Leaders.* The best leaders don't have to search for something significant to do; they are being asked by everyone to join their effort. One of the most effective things we can do is to schedule a lunch or a coffee with a key leader, share our heart with them, and ask them to be a part of it. Don't expect them to fully understand what you're doing or why, but ask them to be a part of exploring and evaluating the process. Starting pilot groups or "test" ministries are some of the best ways to find early adopters.

2. *Give permission.* Permission means letting go and is therefore one of the toughest things to do. However, giving permission to try new things and to think outside of the box can be one of the most empowering things a leader can do. New leaders have breakthrough moments through being empowered. Until we let go, our people will continue to check the box. We also need to give permission for our leaders to stop doing some things:

a. *Permission to stop showing up to every program,* freeing up time to fully vest themselves in their new mission.

b. *Permission to not volunteer on campus,* freeing up time to pioneer ministry outside of the church.

c. *Permission to fail and learn from their failure.* One moment of failure allows a learning opportunity for every group from that point forward.

3. *Protect margin.* We simply cannot ask people to keep adding things to their ministry life. If we do, service will be the first

to go. We have to simplify our forms and find ways to create margin in our current structures. Celebrate addition through subtraction. It's worth the effort to give your people (or yourself) the time to do what you're asking them to do well. Here are some of the greatest ways to protect margin.

a. *Evaluate.* Cut events and projects that don't serve the mission.

b. *Consolidate.* Identify your most effective existing forms and find ways to utilize them as a funnel for discipleship. One example is missional community. If we value community as much as we claim, it is possible to utilize it as a funnel for all things outside the Sunday experience.

c. *Reshape.* If your community groups are your main emphasis outside of the weekend gathering, yet meet the same need only on the micro level, you may need to reshape what your community groups do. Consider adding purposes that can free up other days of the week. This will increase buy-in for each group and increase involvement exponentially.

4. *Find a common language.* The turning point for ANC in creating a structure to support the vision of our church was when we landed on a common language to communicate our vision. Finding a common language requires you to do the necessary groundwork of landing on a structure that supports the vision. Everything we do happens through what we call a Spiritual Formation Funnel and utilizes each biblical calling for communion, mission, and community. Although we discussed these earlier, here's a review:

a. *Expose.* We utilize the Sunday morning worship time (communion) to *expose* relational, physical, and spiritual *need* through Scripture, creative elements, media, and seasonal focus.

b. *Experience.* We utilize a regular scheduled event to help people *experience need* (mission) as a first touch to serving the least. We do this every fifth Sunday, in place of our Sunday morning gathering, communicating priority and creating a safe environment for first-timers to serve in a group setting.

c. *Engage.* We utilize missional/incarnational community to not only build relationships, fellowship, pray, and learn together, but also to *engage need* on a more personal level (in community). Our missional communities are structured to give away as much time as we keep, alternating the focus of each week on biblical community and service.

Authors Hugh Halter and Matt Smay propose that the kingdom becomes most tangible at the intersecting point of community, communion, and mission. This addresses the problem that surfaces when we focus on the three elements independently and forget to overlap them. We work hard to make sure we have a time of communion with God through worship, Bible study, and prayer. We are committed to building community the best we know how in small groups. We are willing to serve regularly in various places.

But it's too easy for those things to exist independently of one another. No wonder we're so busy. Is it possible that the beauty of those things overlapping is not just found in their existence but in their coexistence? As we consider creating a structure to serve the least as a priority of our ministry, we have to think strategically about how community, communion, and mission most naturally overlap.

CREATING A CULTURE OF CHANGE

Recently I came across an online interview with Dr. Karyn Purvis, coauthor of *The Connected Child* and director of the Institute of Child Development at Texas Christian University. She was addressing the orphan crisis in the world and sharing what needs to happen in order to address it. "There are scores of legislators. There are scores of government agencies. There are community services and community agencies. But the real healing, if it's going to happen, it's going to happen in the heart of the church."[14]

Not long ago she was testifying for legislation at our capitol as an invited expert on legislation for foster and adopted children when the senator who chairs the committee said, "This problem is just too, too big for the government. We need the church." Dr. Purvis' response, "And that's my sentiment."[15]

Mine too.

It doesn't stop with the orphan crisis. It extends to poverty across the world. It extends to issues of human trafficking and lack of clean water. It extends to the homeless, to the single mom needing help, and to the neglected widow. And it extends to being hope to our neighbor who may be in perfect health and have more money than you and I combined, but has no hope for eternity.

In order for the church to collectively answer this call, we each have to enter into a time of soul searching. We're going to have to be more aware as individuals. We're going to have to hear God's voice and discern to which part of this challenge God is calling us personally. Is he calling you to make a personal change, to develop a ministry, to engage needs locally or globally, to do an outreach, to adopt, or to foster? We have to be willing to consider anything. It's not about what we want to do. It's about what God wants us to do. When we are faithful to his call, he will align our hearts.

Dr. Purvis offers a handful of thoughts for the church to consider in stewarding these issues. It's bigger than just teaching something new; it's about creating a new church culture.

- We have to cultivate a healing culture—where it's okay to be imperfect.
- We have to become a forgiving culture—where grace is expected and extended.
- We have to create a culture of acceptance—where love is unconditional.
- We have to offer a culture of permission—where we can wait to move until we hear God's voice.[16]

In other words, we have to become more like Jesus.

If we were to cultivate these four things into our church culture, we wouldn't have to worry about the rest. We'd be the church we needed to be. Service to the least would naturally flow out of the grace and compassion of our church culture. It starts with each of us. The church is a collection of Christians either living on mission or avoiding the responsibility.

> If we were to cultivate these four things into our church culture, we wouldn't have to worry about the rest. We'd be the church we needed to be.

If not us, then who? Jesus answers this question on his way into Jerusalem to be crucified. If we remain silent, the rocks themselves will cry out (Luke 19:40). That's a humbling reality that I hope we don't miss. Serving the least is a privilege. It's an honor. And it's an opportunity to serve Jesus himself. His words are clear: "Whatever you did for one of the least of these brothers and sisters of mine, you did for me" (Matthew 25:40). If we don't do it, someone or something else will.

THE JOURNEY

I grew up in a family that loved to fish. Several times a year we would load up the truck at our Colorado home and head to Lake Powell in southern Utah, spending a week or so camping and fishing. One year we woke up in the middle of the night to one of the most incredible storms I've ever seen. It was raining in sheets, with lightning flashing and thunder booming everywhere and wind gusts up to seventy miles per hour. Each of us was standing outside holding a tent post hoping the wind would die down so we could go back into our sleeping bags.

After an hour or so of wrestling with the tent, we loaded up the truck and began the six-hour journey home. I loved going to Lake Powell, but I always hated the trip there and back.

About a month later my dad called me outside to "come and see something." As I rounded the corner I saw the most beautiful thing ever created: a 1972 Winnebago Brave Motor Home. Now, let me paint you a more realistic picture. To a seventh-grade boy, this was awesome. But in the real world it was a thirteen-year-old, twenty-two-foot atrocity with orange couches and brown stripes down the side. It was about as long as it was tall and looked like an oversized mystery machine.

I was in love.

The only thing better than the captain's chairs that swiveled 360 degrees was the awesome eight-track player with the Oak Ridge Boys singing their gospel favorites stuck in the deck.

My life changed that day. I couldn't wait for the next road trip to Lake Powell. It was six hours of switching seats, playing cards, taking naps stretched out on the queen-sized bed, and using the bathroom without having to stop. For the first time, the trip was just as much about the journey as it was the arrival.

When we look at need in the world, when we see the statistics and see millions in need, it's easy to be overwhelmed. We can't stay in ignorance, we must know that it's millions — but we must see it as one: one homeless family off the streets, one orphan finding a home, one hungry mouth fed, one well in Africa dug, one victory at a time, one disciple at a time, one after another, one at a time. We must focus on every mile marker along the way. The journey is not about helping God do something he can't do without us. The journey is about being faithful to Christ. It's about becoming the church that God wants us to be and the church the world needs us to be. It's about being good news to a world in need of good news.

CLOSING THOUGHTS

As you probably figured out by chapter 1, I'm certainly not an academic. I'm a practitioner. I do what I do. That can be good or bad. My hope is that in the case of this book, it's a good thing, and that whatever path it leads you on at the end, you will find Jesus. I'll leave you with a quote from St. Augustine's *De doctrina christiana*. It captures best my hope for you, for me, and my hope for the church.

Whoever, therefore, thinks that he understands the divine Scriptures or any part of them so that it does not build the double love of God and of our neighbor does not understand it at all. Whoever finds a lesson there useful to the building of charity, even though he has not said what the author may be shown to have intended in that place, has not been deceived, nor is he lying in any way. However, if he is deceived in an interpretation which builds up charity, he is deceived in the same way as a man who leaves a road by mistake but passes through a field to the same place toward which the road itself leads.[17]

NOTES

Chapter 1: There's Got to Be More

1. Craig Van Gelder, *The Ministry of the Missional Church: A Community Led by the Spirit* (Grand Rapids: Baker, 2007), 17.

2. Julia Duin, *Quitting Church: Why the Faithful Are Fleeing and What to Do about It* (Grand Rapids: Baker, 2008), 18 (emphasis added).

3. See Shane Claiborne, *The Irresistible Revolution: Living as an Ordinary Radical* (Grand Rapids: Zondervan, 2006), 24.

4. Biblos.com (2004–2010) http://strongsnumbers.com/hebrew/2616.htm (accessed March 23, 2011).

5. Ibid., http://strongsnumbers.com/greek/3628.htm (accessed March 23, 2011).

6. Ibid., http://strongsnumbers.com/hebrew/8199.htm (accessed March 23, 2011).

7. Ibid., http://strongsnumbers.com/greek/1557.htm (accessed March 23, 2011).

8. Merriam-Webster, Inc. (2010) www.merriam-webster.com/dictionary/mercy (accessed March 23, 2011).

9. Ibid., www.merriam-webster.com/dictionary/justice?show=0&t=1288704505 (accessed March 23, 2011).

Chapter 2: A Call and a Response

1. Justin Dillon, *Call and Response: A Film about the World's 27 Million Most Terrifying Secrets* (Fair Trade Fund, 2008).

2. Richard Stearns, *The Hole in Our Gospel* (Nashville: Nelson, 2009), 53.
3. Ibid., 59.
4. Dillon, *Call and Response.*
5. Ibid., 101.
6. Ashley Judd, in *Call and Response: A Film about the World's 27 Million Most Terrifying Secrets* (Fair Trade Fund, 2008): format, DVD.

Chapter 3: Where Gathering and Scattering Collide

1. Richard Rohr, *Hope against Darkness* (Cincinnati: St. Anthony Messenger, 2001), 48.

Chapter 4: Serving through Missional Community

1. Robert Bellah, et al., *Habits of the Heart: Individualism and Commitment in American Life* (Berkeley: Univ. of California Press, 1983), 84.
2. John Howard Yoder, *The Original Revolution: Essays on Christian Pacifism* (Scottdale, PA: Herald, 1977), 30–31.
3. Craig Van Gelder, *The Ministry of the Missional Church: A Community Led by the Spirit* (Grand Rapids: Baker, 2007), 18–19.
4. Ibid., 19.
5. George Barna, *Revolution* (Carol Stream, IL: Tyndale, 2006), 49.
6. Hugh Halter and Matt Smay, *The Tangible Kingdom Primer* (Denver: Missio Publishing, 2009).
7. Reggie McNeil, *Missional Renaissance: Changing the Scorecard for the Church* (San Fransisco: Jossey-Bass, 2009), 140.
8. Darrell L. Guder, *Missional Church: A Vision for the Sending of the Church in North America* (Grand Rapids: Eerdmans, 1998), 153.

Chapter 5: Good News for the Unchurched and Dechurched

1. http://sports.espn.go.com/nfl/columns/story?columnist=mosley_matt&page=hotread1/mosley (accessed October 14, 2010).
2. www.collidemagazine.com/blog/index.php/1452/one-hundred-thirty-million-dollars (accessed March, 28, 2011).

3. www.christianexaminer.com/Articles/Articles%20Dec09/Art_ Dec09_19.html (accessed March 28, 2011).

4. Summarized from Ed Stetzer's blog on evangelism and social justice: www.edstetzer.com/2010/03/monday-is-for-missiology-evang .html (accessed March 15, 2010).

5. Tim Chester and Steve Timmis, *Total Church: A Radical Reshaping around Gospel and Community* (Wheaton, IL: Crossway, 2008), 78–79.

6. Timothy Keller, *Generous Justice: How God's Grace Makes Us Just* (New York: Dutton Adult, 2010), xiv.

7. Tim Keller (Redeemer Vision Paper #1, *The Gospel: Key to Change*) www.redeemer.com/about_us/vision_campaign/resources/ (accessed March 23, 2011).

8. Hugh Halter and Matt Smay, *The Tangible Kingdom: Creating Incarnational Community* (San Francisco: Jossey-Bass, 2008), 42–43.

9. Ibid., 42.

10. Hugh Halter and Matt Smay, *AND: The Gathered and Scattered Church* (Grand Rapids: Zondervan, 2009), 66.

11. http://tatumweb.com/blog/2008/06/05/reveal/ (accessed March 23, 2011).

12. www.abbaconnect.net/for-pastors/greater-impact/ (accessed March 23, 2011).

13. See Darrell L. Guder, *Missional Church: A Vision for the Sending of the Church in North America* (Grand Rapids: Eerdmans, 1998), 128.

14. Ibid., 129.

15. Gabe Lyons, *The Next Christians: The Good News about the End of Christian America* (New York: Doubleday, 2010), 8.

16. www.edstetzer.com/2010/04/monday-is-for-missiology-liber.html (accessed March 23, 2011)

17. Julia Duin, *Quitting Church: Why the Faithful Are Fleeing and What to Do about It* (Grand Rapids: Baker, 2008), 13.

18. Ibid., 20.

19. Reggie McNeil, *Missional Renaissance: Changing the Scorecard for the Church* (San Francisco: Jossey-Bass, 2009), 5.

Chapter 6: Expanding our Understanding of Discipleship

1. Greg Ogden, *Transforming Discipleship: Making Disciples a Few at a Time* (Downers Grove, IL: InterVarsity Press, 2003), ch. 1, "The Discipleship Gap: Where Have All the Disciples Gone?" (www.ivpress.com/title/exc/2388 – 1.pdf), 22 (accessed April 11, 2011).
2. Ibid.
3. Ibid., 23.
4. http://maranathalife.com/lifeline/stats.htm (accessed May 1, 2011).
5. Ogden, *Transforming Discipleship: Making Disciples a Few at a Time*, ch. 1, "The Discipleship Gap: Where Have All the Disciples Gone?" (www.ivpress.com/title/exc/2388 – 1.pdf), 25 – 37 (accessed April 11, 2011).
6. Ibid., 36.
7. www.theintentionaldisciple.com/gpage2.html (accessed April 11, 2011).
8. Ibid.
9. www.theintentionaldisciple.com/gpage.html.html (accessed April 11, 2011).
10. http://www.theintentionaldisciple.com/gpage2.html (accessed April 11, 2011).
11. Craig Van Gelder, *The Ministry of the Missional Church: A Community Led by the Spirit* (Grand Rapids: Baker, 2007), 151.
12. Ogden, *Transforming Discipleship: Making Disciples a Few at a Time*, 37.
13. Darrell L. Guder, *Missional Church: A Vision for the Sending of the Church in North America* (Grand Rapids: Eerdmans, 1998), 130 – 31.
14. www.barna.org/store?page=shop.product_details&flypage= flypage.tpl&category_id=4&product_id=46 (accessed March 23, 2011).

Chapter 7: Embracing the Tension

1. www.charitywater.org/ (accessed March 23, 2011).

2. Craig Van Gelder, *The Ministry of the Missional Church: A Community Led by the Spirit* (Grand Rapids: Baker, 2007), 151.
3. Ibid., 158.
4. www.plantr.org/plantr-podcast—2-who-starts-gospel-movements/ (accessed March 23, 2011).
5. Written by Catalyst; see www.cogun.com/_blog/Bill_Couchenour/ post/The_Tension_Is_Good/ (accessed March 23, 2011); used with permission.

Chapter 8: Partnering with the Nonprofit World

1. Darrell L. Guder, *Missional Church: A Vision for the Sending of the Church in North America* (Grand Rapids: Eerdmans, 1998), 75.
2. Neil Cole, *Church 3.0* (San Francisco: Jossey-Bass, 2010), 53.
3. Ibid., 49.
4. www.freemethodistchurch.org/pdfs/leadership/State_of_the_ Work_2009.pdf (accessed March 23, 2011).

Chapter 9: A New Metric for Success

1. Reggie McNeil, *Missional Renaissance: Changing the Scorecard for the Church* (San Francisco: Jossey-Bass, 2009), 6.
2. David Kinnaman and Gabe Lyons, *Unchristian* (Grand Rapids: Baker, 2007), 226.
3. McNeil, *Missional Renaissance*, 7.
4. www.austinplantr.org (accessed March 23, 2011).
5. See Darrin Patrick and Matt Carter, *For the City: Proclaiming and Living Out the Gospel* (Grand Rapids: Zondervan, 2010).
6. Neal Cole, *Organic Church: Growing Faith Where Life Happens* (San Francisco: Jossey-Bass, 2005), xxiii.
7. www.wdavidphillips.com/measuring-success-in-ministry (accessed March 23, 2011).
8. www.backyardmissionary.com/2008/06/re-imagining-success. html (accessed March 23, 2011).

Chapter 10: Becoming a Barefoot Church

1. www.loganleadership.com/2010/09/missio-intensive-day – 1 .html (accessed October 1, 2010).
2. Neil Cole, *Church 3.0* (San Fransisco: Jossey-Bass, 2010), 56.
3. www.quotationcollection.com/author/Albert_Schweitzer/quotes (accessed March 22, 2011).
4. Alan Hirsch and Dave Ferguson, *On the Verge: The Future of the Church as Apostolic Movement* (Grand Rapids: Zondervan 2011), 54.
5. Greg Ogden, *Transforming Discipleship: Making Disciples a Few at a Time* (Downers Grove, IL: InterVarsity Press, 2003), ch. 1, "The Discipleship Gap: Where Have All the Disciples Gone?" (www.ivpress.com/title/exc/2388 – 1.pdf), 21 (accessed September 21, 2010).
6. Stuart Murray: *Church after Christendom* (Portland: Paternoster, 2005), 19.
7. Ibid., 20.
8. Craig Van Gelder, *The Ministry of the Missional Church: A Community Led by the Spirit* (Grand Rapids: Baker, 2007), 167.
9. Ibid., 169 – 70.
10. Ibid., 170.
11. Ibid., 171.
12. Ibid.
13. Ibid.
14. Dr. Karyn Purvis, http://vimeo.com/13835491 (accessed October 20, 2010).
15. Ibid.
16. Ibid.
17. As quoted in Scot McKnight, *A Community Called Atonement: Living Theology* (Nashville: Abingdon, 2007), 142.